SO NOW YOU'RE A *Widow*

SO NOW YOU'RE A *Widow*

Tips, Advice, and Stories from
WIDOWS *to* WIDOWS

Bonnie Merryfield

outskirts
press

Table of Contents

Dedication

To my husband, Peter:

My greatest joy in life was being your wife. This book is for you, sweetheart. You always gave me the confidence to pursue whatever goal I wanted to reach. Your encouragement was felt throughout the writing of this book, and I hope I made you proud. I'll love you always. Keep those signs that you're still watching over us coming!

Acknowledgments

To my family and friends, especially my treasured girl-friends (the best support system in the world!)—You never lost faith that I would successfully accomplish this project. You patiently listened to me discuss my book when someone asked about it, even after hearing me passionately describe its contents too many times to count!

To Susan—Thank you from the bottom of my heart for reading and critiquing the chapters as I finished writing them. You're my hero. You're a warrior, Susan, fighting your cancer while supporting your husband in his own battle with the disease. I'm so blessed to have you in my life, my friend.

To Joleen—You were my first interview. Thank you for your insights and honesty and for helping me fine-tune my interviewing technique!

To Karoleen—Your suggestion to add the journal section at the end of each chapter was the frosting on the cake!

To Ira and Scott, my "Techwise" computer techs—Thank you for always taking the time to patiently answer and explain my computer questions. I couldn't have done this without you!

To Riley and Murphy, my precious cats—Thank you for insisting I take much-needed breaks from my writing for petting, treats, and playtime. You knew I needed those breaks even when I didn't. You're a constant source of joy and comfort to me!

Last, but not least—The biggest "thank you" to the women I interviewed who shared their wisdom and opened their hearts to help others. This is your book as much as it is mine. Our in-depth interviews included tears and laughter, and through it all we paid tribute to our husbands with what we were accomplishing. Bless you all.

Introduction

When we recited our marriage vows, we were too caught up in the excitement of the moment to give even a fleeting thought as to how our lives would change if "'til death do us part" became a reality. And then the unthinkable happened. Our husband's death either occurred suddenly or was somehow expected due to health issues. You'll hear well-meaning people say one way is "better" than the other, but I don't agree with that statement. Suddenly or expected, death is death. The men we loved and shared our lives with are gone either way, and we've become widowed.

We've met with the funeral home and ordered the urn or casket, prayer cards, copies of death certificates, condolence books for signing, and thank-you cards. We've written or proofed the obituary and may have been surprised at the cost to have it printed in the newspaper. We've planned and carried out the funeral and arranged for a casual or formal reception following the service. We've been consoled by family and friends and were grateful for their support; we've even consoled others who were grieving our loss. However, at some point, we find ourselves alone, and our new lives as widowed women have begun.

For years, I had subconsciously watched family members and friends who had been widowed, having no idea at the time how much this would help me when I eventually found myself in their position. I am truly fortunate to have these women as my role models.

There was so much I didn't know when I was widowed, so much I thought I was the only one experiencing, and that's why I decided to write this book. Women who have been recently widowed, or even those who have been widowed for a time, need to know everything they're experiencing is normal and has been experienced in one form or another by other women.

When I contacted the thirty-four women who contributed to this book and asked them to participate, all were thrilled to share what they felt other widowed women needed to know. They said there was so much they hadn't known or anticipated and wanted to ease the way for others.

This book is the work of a community of widowed women, and while none of us aspired to be part of it, we hope you'll find the experiences we're sharing to be helpful. We may not be with you physically, but imagine yourself sitting in a cozy room surrounded by caring women who want to share with you what they've learned.

So Now You're a Widow...Tips, Advice, and Stories from Widows to Widows is intended primarily for widowed women over the age of fifty, although much will apply to those of all ages. Each chapter contains tips, advice, and stories from widowed women in that age group.

According to the U.S. Census Bureau, nearly 700,000 women lose their husbands each year, and one-half of these women have been widowed by age sixty-five; the 2017 Statista Portal of Statistics, using 22,500 different sources, found the U.S. was home to approximately 11.64 million widows.

However, behind the impersonal statistics are real women, with real-life stories, among them the women who eagerly have agreed to share with you what they've learned or experienced. The thirty-four women interviewed had so much they wanted to contribute that interviews averaged three hours. We may not cover everything you feel you need to know, but every woman reading this book will find something she can relate to, something that will assist, motivate, comfort, or reassure her.

This isn't a book that you need to read from beginning to end. Glance at the titles and subtitles of the chapters. Choose the chapter that interests you, and decide when you feel up to reading all or even part of it. After each chapter's introduction, you'll hear from the women interviewed.

You'll notice I've referred to those about to be quoted as "women who have been widowed" instead of "the widows." There's a specific reason for that. Being a widow is part of who they are, but it's not their entire identity. They're still the multifaceted women they were before the heartbreak of losing a husband—certainly a life-changing experience, but one that has contributed to making them the strong women they are. There are commonalities in what they have to say but also opinions and experiences as unique as each woman. Their quotes have not been edited because I

wanted to capture the purity and honesty of their responses to questions which centered on my chapter topics.

As you read their comments, you'll notice, occasionally,
that some of the women have less to say on a topic than
others. I included the shorter responses since in any discussion with many women— and remember, you want to imagine yourself sitting in a cozy room with a group of caring
women—there are those who sometimes have a lot to say
and others who don't. Those shorter comments are every
bit as important as the longer ones in allowing you to experience various viewpoints and experiences or to get an idea
of how many women felt the same about a specific topic.

At the end of each chapter, you'll find a journal section
for you to write your thoughts on the subject we covered,
almost as if you're taking part in the discussion with the
women. Your honest answers will help you to process what
you've just read and, hopefully, further your own healing. In
the back of this book are brief descriptions of the women
who opened their hearts to share with you what they've
learned. If you're reading a chapter and are curious about
the woman quoted, you'll be able to discover a little more
about her. The first names and last initials they've asked
me to use are arranged alphabetically. The women I interviewed live throughout the country and are from all walks
of life and all rungs of the socioeconomic ladder.

As you read the following pages, remember that the love
and memories you shared with your husband will always be
with you. Death can't take those away. Now it's time to hold

them close within your heart and rebuild your life. Yes, it's easier for some than for others, but you're stronger than you think. You can come through this. We have faith in you!

Before we move on to the following chapters, I'd like to explain how I entered into widowhood by sharing what my husband Peter and I experienced as our battle with his health issues reached its conclusion.

Pete valiantly fought myelodysplastic syndrome, MDS, for seven years, from his diagnosis in 2011 until he passed on May 15, 2018. MDS was once referred to as "pre-leukemia" and occurs when bone marrow produces defective red blood cells, cells that contribute to a person's energy and oxygen. One of the first symptoms is extreme fatigue, and the disease is diagnosed through blood tests. As Pete's disease progressed, there were various forms of treatments, including Procrit injections, transfusions, and chemotherapy. Years later, my once "picture of health" Pete developed congestive heart failure, CHF.

We were together every day following his diagnosis, and Pete often said, "I couldn't do this without you." It's beyond difficult to see the man you love struggling to survive, but I discovered, as many of you have, that I was stronger than I ever imagined and simply did what had to be done.

The most concise way for me to describe the end of our seven-year journey in battling these diseases is to share two updates, the last of many emailed to family and friends. The first update was to prepare them for the inevitable, and the second was to notify them of Pete's passing. Pete was such a special person. His warm smile was contagious, and people gravitated to his fun-loving personality. In many of the following chapter introductions, you'll learn more about us as I share what I've learned since I became widowed.

Second-to-Last Update Sent to Family & Friends

May 13, 2018

Dearest Family & Friends,

This evening Pete was transported to Hope Hospice here in Ft. Myers. No more black and blue arms and stomach from all the needles, no more intrusive tests, no more being coaxed by CNAs and RNs to eat or drink when it didn't matter anymore. Pete will be kept comfortable and free from pain at this blessed place. That's what all of us who love him want for him.

Pete has been an inspiration for so many and has fought so hard since he was first diagnosed with MDS in 2011 and then CHF in 2014. He's undergone sixty transfusions, literally hundreds of blood draws, the 2016 summer clinical trial at Moffatt Cancer Center in Tampa, weekly Procrit shots, and three different kinds of chemo, one of which nearly took his life last summer. He's also endured painful (and futile) shots in his neck and back at a pain management clinic. Since last summer, Pete's been hospitalized five times and had three stays in rehabilitation centers.

So much of what he loved doing was being taken away from him, bit by bit. He hadn't been able to drive since the end of June 2017, when he was given the last chemo doctors could give him for the MDS. Following that chemo, he was forced to use a walker or wheelchair. He wasn't able to golf as he so enjoyed doing with his fun foursome. He could no longer walk with me in the morning. Our friends Mya and Sandy were kind enough to loan us their electric scooter, and smiling Pete, with a bottle of water in the scooter's basket, could once again accompany me as I walked; he loved that, not just for the degree of independence it gave him but because we were outside together, and Pete, being a "people person," was able to visit with those who would stop him to say "hi." That pleasure, too, ended when his condition worsened. He was too weak to do any boating, and we sold our boat last summer. Pete loved socializing and going out to lunch with his group of friends called the "Romeos" (Retired Old Men Eating Out). He had looked forward to that all last summer while he was in rehab, but that pleasure was taken away as well.

During his last six-week rehab stay, we were in the rehab dining room, and he told me he'd "really enjoy a drink," but that was out of the question. He missed his two cats, Riley and Murphy, and his favorite couch, where he'd get comfortable to watch TV. His world had shrunk to one of doctor visits, hospitals, and rehab facilities, yet he never complained. This latest hospitalization began on the day he was to have returned home after being away for two months. All he had gained in six weeks of intense rehab, following three weeks of hospitalization, was wiped out.

Last Sunday he developed severe otitis with pus, an ear infection and inflammation. Because his hearing was dramatically affected, I'd write him notes to explain what was happening to him. These last few days Pete has stopped eating and drinking. When the nurses tried to give him meds, for the first time he refused to open his mouth.

Yesterday Dr. Olga Freeman, our primary doctor, said Pete's kidney and liver counts were better, as were his ears. However, his body isn't better; it's simply tired of fighting. He may open his eyes for a few seconds, but he's sleeping almost all the time.

We know God has everyone's "Go-To-Heaven" date circled on His calendar, and I agree with the doctors that Pete's date is not far away. I've volunteered at AngelsGrace Hospice for nine and a half years and can finally acknowledge the signs that he will soon be leaving us.

You've all been such a strong support system for both of us. I've read your cards, notes, and emails to Pete, and they've made him smile to hear how much he means to so many. You'll never know how your loving calls and visits kept us going on days when we really needed them. You've brought me meals, fed the cats, and even scheduled "play dates" to keep them from getting too lonely when I've been with Pete all day. My in-laws, Pete's brother Terry and his wife Marcia, have run errands and kept us company at the hospital and rehab. Terry even took me car shopping when I unexpectedly needed to replace our Florida car. Tomorrow Marcia is going to the funeral home with me to make final arrangements. Who would have dreamed when Pete and I came down here on November 8th that I would be doing this?

Please pray that Pete's final journey will be pain-free and peaceful. He is such a truly good person, as you all know. No one has ever heard him say a negative word about anyone. He would always make excuses for a person or find something positive to say.

If you would, maybe pray, too, that I'll find the strength to do everything that these next days will require of me.

Love,

Bonnie

Final Update Sent to Family and Friends

March 15, 2018

Dear Family & Friends,

This morning at 4:43 Kimberly, an RN at Hope Hospice, called to gently inform me Pete passed away very peacefully at 4:40 A.M. I had prayed before bed that the Lord would take Pete to his heavenly home without any more suffering. And He did.

When Terry, Marcia, and I entered his room to say our goodbyes, Pete was covered with a quilt made by hospice volunteers; prominently displayed in the middle of the quilt were a regal-looking lion and lioness. Big cats. How fitting for a cat-lover. I was given the beautiful quilt to take home with me. It's now on our bed, and Riley and Murphy are sleeping on top of it.

Love, Bonnie

CHAPTER 1
Your Source of Inner Strength

You Don't Have to Go Through This Alone

Each of us has our own belief system that supports us, giving hope, strength, and comfort in difficult times. I fought for Pete to recover every step of the way, but believing in a loving God helped get me through Pete's deteriorating health, especially that last tumultuous year of hospitals, rehab facilities, and, finally, hospice. Pete would rally but never to where he had been before the latest health crisis. I had always been a sound sleeper; my head would hit the pillow, and I'd be out like a light. That changed as Pete's disease took its toll on both of us. When I'd wake in the middle of the night, I knew God was awake, too, and I'd pray and talk to Him, asking Him to do what was best for Pete. When we were in Wisconsin, Father John and Deacon Mike would visit Pete in the hospital and rehab and bring him Communion, a source of strength and comfort to both of us.

Near the end, in Florida, I'm not sure if Pete was aware of Father Lawrence giving him the Last Rites, but I'd like to think he was. I do know those of us in Pete's hospital room heard the words and were comforted. I'm so thankful I had arranged for Father Lawrence to come that afternoon because at the time I had no idea Pete would be entering Hope Hospice later that same evening. When Pete passed in hospice thirty-two hours later, my brother-in-law Terry, sister-in-law Marcia, and I went to say our goodbyes just as the sun was rising. At the foot of Pete's hospice bed, there was a narrow table, and on it was the Bible (opened to one of my favorite verses "The 23rd Psalm"), a lighted candle, a porcelain angel, and a vase filled with vibrant red roses. Pete was covered with a beautiful quilt handmade by hospice volunteers, and the spacious room was filled with peace, love, and tranquility.

The funeral service in Florida was held at St. John XXIII and in Wisconsin at St. Anthony on the Lake; both religious ceremonies were lovely and comforting, and, as my Irish relatives would say, "Pete had a good send-off." In rereading this, I'm noticing how many times I've used the word "comfort" in one form or another, and that's what my Catholic faith is to me, comforting.

My faith, together with the love of family and friends, supported and strengthened me before I lost my husband and continues to do so. I believe every day is a gift from God, who is with us always, and I thank Him for being there to help me get through all the days ahead without Pete.

Many of you have already found your own source of inner strength. The experiences shared by other women who have been widowed may offer options you haven't yet considered to provide emotional support as you begin your journey. You'll also read in their honest reflections that sometimes their source of strength wasn't where they had expected it to be.

"If you're a person of faith, use the fact that the Lord is watching out for you and has a plan for you. If you're not a person of faith, you can attend a grief bereavement group at a church or synagogue even if you're not a member there. I didn't exactly get my inner strength from my faith. It was my own inner strength and the support of family and friends." Barb W.

"If you're alone, try a bereavement group through your church, a hospital, or hospice. I gained much of my strength from my religion and from friends and didn't feel I needed additional support from a bereavement group." Barb B.

"When you're ready, purchase some books on grieving with a Christian theme. You need the joy of the Lord at this time, and that's what helped me—my personal relationship with the Lord. I'm a Christian, and that's what gave me strength." Beverly K.

"You find your inner strength wherever you can because there's no alternative. You have to do what you have to do." Pearl G.

"I believe in prayer. Give your problems to the Lord. The hardest thing was, and is, going to church without my husband because we had a closeness in church, and we'd hold hands. Now I listen to church services on my iPad." Carol L.

"Writing in a journal really helped me while he was ill, and I kept writing in it after he died. Sometimes I feel I'm not religious enough. I've had many tragic losses and have told God that I've had enough 'doors' being closed." Marijo Z.

"I had people say to me, 'Oh, you're so strong!' but I have no idea where that strength came from." Jan B.

"Do what feels right for you. When my husband died, I followed traditional Jewish funeral traditions, but even though the Jewish religion means something to me, I don't go to temple regularly." Lyn L.

"My husband and I would go to church on special occasions. After he passed, I began going every Sunday and sat with friends. Having a routine worked for me. I found an inner strength I didn't know I had." Jolene M.

"Religion was and is a strong factor in providing my inner strength." Karen C.

"I've always been a Christian. When you have confidence in Christ, He is with you all the time, and you're never alone. I was raised Methodist and later became a Presbyterian. When I was younger, a woman at church told me, 'God is Love.' I've never forgotten that." Audrey C.

"I have a strong faith that has helped me." Joan A.

"None of my ability to reach out to others or to cope with my own grief would have been possible without my

4

strong faith in God. That faith has helped me cope with the loss of two husbands, as well as the loss of my parents at an early age and the loss of my seven brothers, a niece and a nephew who passed away with an incurable congenital disease which I now have. My God is so real to me that I feel He is always by my side when I need Him or when I want to thank Him. My prayers for help may not be answered in the way I had thought or hoped, but God always answered my every need in His time and according to His way, which is better than I could have dreamed. I feel so blessed to have this special relationship with my God. It has always been a part of my life, and I consider it to be the very greatest gift of my 'almost' ninety years!" Gladi B.

"I have a good faith, which helps." Ruby C.

"The power of God gave me the strength to stay with my dying husband all day, every day. I felt God was protecting him. While driving the long distance to be with my husband, I prayed to God to keep me safe because my husband needed me. Now, I ask myself, 'How did I do that?' Later, I decided I had to have had Guardian Angels watching over me." Mary B.

"My faith gave me strength. I'm a communicant and went to church every day. Without faith, I don't think I could have survived dealing with the many impersonal medical professionals I came into contact with. The hardest prayer you'll ever say is 'Lord, if You can't heal him, then take him.' There is no 'why?' The Lord decides the 'why.' Remember, caregivers can get caught in the avalanche when things are crumbling around the dying person." Evelyn C.

"I'm not tied to any one religion, but I am spiritual. I'm still looking for strength even though my kids have helped me a great deal." Sandy G.

"Faith is a strong factor in my life, and it's very important to me." Judie N.

"I depended upon God to get me through my loss, and my faith is still strong. Sometimes, my pride tells me I can get through it alone, but I can't." Lou H.

"Yes, faith helped a lot at the time. However, even though I still have faith, it's hard to go to church. I still get weepy. A friend said it's because I feel church is a safe place where I can let my emotions out. I still can get emotional with church music, music we listened to together or had at our wedding." Kay J.

"Religion didn't help me much in the beginning after my husband died. He was Catholic, and I converted from my family's Methodist faith when I married him. After he died, I went back to the Methodist church, and now I'm an active member." Nancy J.

"After my husband died, I went to church, and when I walked in, I felt peace. I knew he was in Heaven. A lady I knew had to go to a different church after her husband died." Ginny G.

"I believe in God and the hereafter. It's the way I was raised, to live your faith. I've always been a strong person." Shirley W.

"My Catholic faith helped me 100 percent. I truly believe you have to pray. My prayer was 'Please, God, don't let him suffer anymore.' If I hadn't had faith, I couldn't have made it, and my faith remains strong. I think your faith grows stronger after you lose someone." Kathy H.

"If I didn't know he was in Heaven waiting for me, I couldn't get out of bed in the morning. I feel God drew my husband back to his faith, and my faith grew through his illness." Joyce B.

"I have faith, but I can't say it got me through my loss. Thank goodness, I had the support system of friends, because my family lived out of state. I had to keep it together for my teenage son. It's very difficult for me to verbalize religion, but I knew my religion was there if I needed it." Joanne W.

"Of course, faith in God helped me! I have an unbelievable faith in Christianity. You don't have to go to church. I had many conversations with God on my walks. My husband passed his strength on to me." Angie O.

"I'm Catholic, but my religion didn't really help. I did pray, though, that my husband would have an easy exit. Then I felt guilty about that because I wasn't praying for him to get well, even though I knew there was no hope he'd recover. I was so busy with working and trying to keep him comfortable that I just did what had to be done." Lila S.

"I'm very active in the Methodist church. I have many friends there—girlfriends and couples—and confided in people. There's no way I could have come through my loss without my faith." Kay P.

"My family gave me my strength. My faith didn't help all that much." Debbi C.

"I'm a strong person, and my inner strength came from within. I'm pretty much alone. For a while, I was kind of mad at God and would ask how could He let this happen to my husband." Lee M.

"My spiritual belief in an afterlife helped me. I knew my husband was happy where he was. I have to say that my cats, who were grieving right along with me, provided great comfort and, yes, strength during this time." Bobbi V.

And a final thought:

"Years ago, a Catholic grade school principal signed his papers with this quote: 'Life is like an unsharpened pencil. Without God, it has no point.' This quote helped me when my sixty-nine-year-old husband passed away from lung cancer three days after being told to get his affairs in order. It is still helping me all these years later. Because of our Catholic faith, after he passed, I knew my husband was no longer suffering and was at peace with the Lord, which gave me great comfort. My husband was a good, loving, faith-filled man, so I was certain that he was in Heaven with God. His death was meaningful as all of us there were praying the Rosary as he passed. May God bless every woman going through such a difficult time." Sherry J.

Ask yourself—

After reading this chapter, "Your Source of Inner Strength," what were my immediate thoughts?

_____

_____

_____

_____

_____

Was there something that made a special impression on me?

_____

_____

_____

_____

What gave me my inner strength before my husband passed?

_____

_____

_____

_____

What gave me inner strength after he passed?

_____

_____

_____

_____

_____

What unexpected sources of strength did I discover?

_____

_____

_____

_____

_____

What advice would I give to someone who is in need of a source of inner strength?

_____

_____

_____

_____

_____

How might I try to increase my inner strength?

_____

_____

_____

_____

_____

What I want to remember from this chapter:

_____

_____

_____

_____

_____

CHAPTER 2
Grieving

"It Will Come in Waves, but Eventually, the Waves Become Further Apart."

The first thing you need to do is not to listen to anyone who wants to tell you how to grieve. They are not you, and your husband was yours, not theirs. There is no grief timeline for when you should start, how you should do it, and when you should stop. Now that we've gotten that out of the way, let me share some things with you.

My dear friend Joanne lost her husband to a sudden heart attack on the first night of their Florida vacation with their seventeen-year-old son. Joanne later said to me, "People can tell you to take it one day at a time, but sometimes it's one hour at a time." Someone told her, "Grief comes in waves, but eventually, the waves will become further apart." That really made an impression on me.

Immediately after losing Pete, I was so grateful that he was no longer suffering and so busy that grieving had to sit on the back burner until I had time to deal with it. We were at our condo in Florida, and there were eleven days

12

between Pete's passing and the day I was scheduled to fly home to Wisconsin, a trip home that had been rescheduled twice before due to his fluctuating condition. There was so much to be done: planning the Florida funeral and reception, choosing poster photos to be displayed, packing and mailing Pete's Florida wardrobe to Wisconsin, beginning to make all those calls to the bank, social security, insurance companies, financial institutions, canceling his future medical and physical therapy appointments. As new widows, our tasks may have been different, but we all had tasks that needed to be accomplished.

When I flew home with our two cats, our ginger tabby Riley and our gray tabby Murphy, I was grateful to have my Florida in-laws Terry and Marcia to help me. Walking into our Wisconsin home wasn't as difficult for me as you might think. Pete had spent a large portion of the previous summer in hospitals and rehabs, so I'd been alone at home during that time.

However, I think the cats expected him to be at the house. They had accepted his absence from the condo because he hadn't been back there for over two months, but the house was a different story. After being released from their cat carriers, Riley and Murphy ran upstairs and downstairs looking for Pete, and when they couldn't find him in his usual places, seeing their confusion broke my heart. Even so, I felt our home, which we had built forty-three years earlier, greeting me with the love that had always filled it.

It rained heavily during the Wisconsin funeral service, which was attended by almost 300 friends and family. As the service ended and we left the church, the rain stopped, and a brilliant sun shone in the now-blue sky.

Many of those who had been at the church came to the casual reception at our home and brought large quantities of delicious food; people were inside throughout the house, outside on the screened-in porch, and in the backyard under canopies. It was a reminder to everyone of the many fun get-togethers we had had at our home throughout the years.

We positioned Pete's large portrait from the funeral behind the bar, where he used to hold court at our parties, and five of his buddies poured a glass of his favorite Bombay gin and set it out "for Pete." Later in the afternoon they said, "Well, we know Bonnie won't drink this, so we'll pass it around until it's gone." This warm, Irish-wake-type gathering was something Pete would have loved, and it was a perfect way for our Wisconsin friends who had not been with us those last difficult months in Florida to say goodbye to him.

Then the Busy Time was over, friends and family had returned home, and it was just Riley, Murphy, and I. Sleep wasn't easy to come by, even with the cats cuddled up on either side of me. When I couldn't sleep, I'd turn on the TV and watch Hallmark movies, read, or start cleaning out Pete's chest of drawers.

My grief really hit me in the middle of one sleepless night as I held his most recent wallet containing his driver's license, insurance and club membership cards, and little personal items. There was even a four-leaf clover that our friend John had given Pete for "good luck." That all brought on the tears, as did seeing the eyeglasses he would never again wear.

Then I remembered what had gotten me through the time right after Pete passed, and I again allowed myself to feel his presence. Oh, of course, I knew his physical body was gone, but I truly felt, and feel to this day, that he's still watching over those he loved and who loved him. His picture is next to my bed, and I say, "Good morning, sweetheart. Love you. Start the day!" the first words we'd say to each other every morning. At night, I say, "Night, sweetheart. Love you," the last words we'd say to each other before we'd go to sleep.

I still have moments of sadness driving past the "Bag Drop," where I'd "deposit" Pete with his golf club bag to meet Gene, Rich, and Bob, his foursome buddies, or when I'm looking for greeting cards and see the "Husband" section. The first time a receptionist at a new doctor's office asked if I was married or single, I had to pause for a moment before I answered, "Widowed," because that hadn't been one of the choices, and it felt strange to answer, "Single." That was an unexpected moment of sadness eleven months after Pete passed.

There will always be little Shots of Grief when you and I least expect them, but we can deal with those as they come. We learn to acknowledge them and move on because that's what we have to do.

My advice is to let yourself grieve but continue to live. Confide in a trusted friend or family member when you feel the need. Those who love you will understand you can't be brave all the time.

Hospitals, hospices, and churches offer bereavement groups, something you might want to consider attending. Grief counseling, both group and one-on-one, is also available for those adjusting to their loss. There is help available, and you don't have to go through this alone.

Other women who have been widowed have dealt with the grieving process, and their insights and experiences may help you with yours.

"The way you grieve is uniquely your own. I didn't care for any of the books on grief that I read. As a matter of fact, I found them depressing and dismissed them because they were making my wounds raw." Pearl G.

"Don't listen to anyone. Until someone has gone through losing a husband, they can't know, don't know. I actually think you're going through a type of PTSD (post-traumatic stress disorder). Sometimes it's the little things that get you. I opened the coat closet, saw his coat, and just sobbed. You need to allow yourself to understand and accept that whatever you feel is how you feel. Does that make sense? A friend who had lost her husband told me she thought the second year is harder than the first. She said the first year you're just numb and dealing with the legal stuff and everything else that has to be done. In our culture it's hard to grieve when you're busy meeting with your attorney, for instance. The second year you realize this is the way it's going to be from now on; he's not coming back. You develop 'widow's brain,' where it's hard to focus on things. You're foggy. I was only able to read, which I love doing, after a year and a half had passed. I went to grief counseling a few times but stopped because I felt uncomfortable and, at times, felt I was 'counseling' the group leader." Joyce B.

"I read a book on grieving that said there were no rules for grief. Each of us grieves in a different way. Two weeks after my husband died, I went back to work, and on the way home one day, I just cried. However, work did help me. When I'd get home, I'd turn on the radio so it wouldn't be so quiet. I joined Curves to exercise. I'd also walk the bike trail, and I'd cry. I remembered my husband joking and saying to bury him along the bike trail so I'd see him every day." Ginny G.

"Don't be afraid to cry in front of friends; getting it out makes you feel better. You have to take time to do your crying. For me, it sometimes helped. I, personally, didn't go to a grief support group. It made me feel sadder. At first, you're so busy that there's no time to dwell on your loss. Things can set you off, like a movie. I cried over something seven years later." Lee M.

"Grieving is a slow process. At first, it's hard. It fades, but every so often it hits you—a song, a place, a movie on sailboats (we had a sailboat) can trigger it. I go to his grave and that of my relatives', put wreaths on the graves, and say prayers. In the beginning my family was nearby and called or stopped over every day and helped me. After a year, I was on my own, and that's when I became active in my church. It's still lonesome. There are happy memories and some sad. You don't really ever get over it. You carry on and go on to new adventures. I have friends who invited me to a Super Bowl party nearby. After he passed, I joined Young Timers at the Boy Scout headquarters where I had worked. It's a group for those who were active in scouting, and I enjoy it." Nancy J.

"Everyone grieves differently and has her own way of getting through grief. You can listen to advice, but don't let them push." Kay J.

"It never seems to go away. Try to get out and do things. It helps to have family around. Now I have no family nearby, and it's harder because I'm totally alone. Others have things to do, and that leaves me alone." Jan B.

"Let it be. Keep breathing. Believe that the Holy Spirit is with you with every breath you take. You're not alone. I have faith that my husband and I will have our reunion in Heaven. The hardest thing is when you have an experience that you want to share with him. At times you just ache. You never know when it will hit." Audrey C.

"Grieving is forever. I think people who don't have faith have a more difficult time getting through it. I was a hospice nurse and saw that. It's good to talk through grief with friends, and I've been blessed with good kids. Think of the good times you had, and that will overcome the bad. The dash between his birth date and the date he died is most important, how he lived his life, not the dates themselves." Carol L.

"The waves of grief do get further apart as time goes on. You're heading to a shore, and you have to swim and, at times, tread water to get to that shore. You can't let the grief pull you under. You might need help to reach that shore, and you might not know where you'll end up. Keep going. Don't believe those who say, 'Give it time. Time heals all wounds.' It doesn't without you making an effort. You have to open your heart and mind to the fact that you can move on. I believe, and have seen, people who don't want to heal, who like where they are, who thrive on pity from others, who keep dredging up their loss to get that pity." Barb W.

"If you're grieving, it means you probably had a great relationship. The way you feel will improve as time goes on, but you have to work at getting through it. There will be happy times and sad times." Debbi C.

"It's a rough ride, but go along with it. Accept the ups and downs. Give yourself permission to grieve. Grieving is an individual process. When you think of your husband, and the thought of him brings more smiles than tears, you'll know your grief is easing. I had worked in the funeral business, which helped me deal with loss. You'll always grieve, but if after a year you're not progressing, get professional help. You could be experiencing what is called 'valid guilt' over something. The funeral home, hospital, or hospice can refer you to a bereavement group or counselor, and that might help you work through it. There's also something called 'lonely hearts' grief, where a surviving spouse stops living because she never worked to get past her grief." Bobbi V.

"You'll get through it, but you'll never forget. I had an inner strength that God would get me through it. Mostly, I had to work through it myself. I'm relatively independent. Keeping in contact with friends and the ability to get out helped me, as did traveling." Barb B.

"That quote about grief coming in waves, but eventually the waves become further apart, is true. Everyone grieves differently. When my husband was sick for so long and then died, I first felt relief; then the grief hit me. I also felt anger that maybe we could have avoided this. Then there was acceptance." Lila S.

"It's not going to last forever. I cried every day for three months, then went one day, then two, then three days without crying. I think the real pain comes after two months. Before that, you're numb. We all have periods of grief, but as time goes on, they don't last as long. When I'd be in the shower, my husband would knock on the shower door and say, 'Cabana (boy), here. Do you need a towel?' I was in the shower three months after he died, heard him saying that, and started to cry. I don't think you ever stop grieving." Beverly K.

"Grieving is a never-ending process. Ten years later I don't have as many breakdowns as before. Anyone who has lost a husband will find her own path. A lot depends on how good a marriage you had." Angie O.

"You have to let yourself feel bad. Someone told me that quote about grief coming in waves, and that's true. I went years without shedding a tear. Then I opened his wallet, saw his driver's license, and started to cry. I didn't pay attention to the stages-of-grief books; they did nothing for me, gave me no comfort. But some women may find comfort reading them." Joanne W.

"There's no Death 101 class on what you can do or not do. My advice is each day put one foot in front of the other. Take it a day at a time. Everyone comes in the beginning, but then that slows down. That's because people go on with their lives, but yours has stopped. The Cancer Center set up one-on-one grief counseling for me. My grief counselor told me, 'That Number One hole in your heart will always be there, but the tight grip on your heart will loosen over time.' I asked her, 'How is a widow supposed to look, how is she supposed to act?' My car was my safe place. I would get in and just drive. But I had to be careful of 'Widow's Fog.' One day I ended up in a dangerous part of Chicago, totally lost. I called one of my sons, who got out a map (this was before GPS) and directed me out of that area." Kathy H.

"I didn't really grieve after my husband died. I grieved while he was alive because of what he was going through.

I'm thankful he didn't have to suffer. It was a beautiful death." Shirley W.

"It took several years for my grief to lessen, but it never really goes away. It just gets less painful. I still get waves of grief. Two months after my husband died, I joined a widows/widowers group at church. It's a great group of people. I could talk more to them, and they allowed me to express my grief." Lou H.

"I suggest you call friends to see how they're doing. Reach out to others." Judie N.

"I'm still grieving thirteen years later. He has missed many life milestones that I would have loved sharing with him. It took a long time to overcome the feeling of grief, especially at church. That surprised me many times when I thought a church service should be helping me." Sherry J.

"People say, 'Get over it!' a lot. Don't listen to them. You have to work through the grief. I took a bereavement class and that helped, as did reading a lot of books on the stages of grief. I didn't have much time to grieve because I had four kids to support. I had to run our liquor store; owning that store had been a dream of his. Operating it felt like I was continuing that dream." Marijo Z.

"It's good to grieve. Everyone grieves in her own time and in her own way. Grieving goes on longer than you think it will. It gets easier, but you never, ever, ever lose it. I held it in, and no one saw me cry because I did my grieving privately. Get it off your shoulders; it's healthy to let the grief out. Church helped me an awful lot. I looked forward to going. I went to the crypt every week and talked to him. He was my only love. A song would make me cry; certain things still trigger the grief. Nine years later my heart still breaks." Mary B.

"Do it in your own time. No one can tell you what that time is. Don't be hard on yourself. There should be no 'should's' in your vocabulary. You experience grief in stages. You need to feel grief when you're ready. You're so exhausted from what you've been through. I went into a room to grieve because I needed solitude. I called it 'going into a cave to lick my wounds.' Find a safe space and 'let be.'" Evelyn C.

"There's no timeline for grief; do it in your own time. The grief is always there, and the pain will come back. You can turn to religion, cry, or do nothing. People told me to take my own time. There were times I'd be very busy, and then there were quiet times." Sandy G.

"I never cried until he died. Grieving is normal. It's crummy, but it's your new normal." Karen C.

"I remember feeling overwhelmed." Carole C.

"I lost three family members—my father, an aunt and uncle—within seven months before losing my husband, and I couldn't cry anymore. My mother-in-law was in a senior care facility, and I had to take care of her every day. I checked on her care, wrote checks for her, everything my husband had done. I was the one who had to tell her he had died, and I had to make his funeral arrangements while sitting with her. It took a week before I broke down and cried for my loss." Lyn L.

"I can cry anytime. It's only been nine months." Joan A.

"Situations will be different. When I lost my first husband, my childhood sweetheart and the father of my four children, I had no time to grieve. We had just arrived in London that day for his job. We had lived two years in Australia and had sold our house in the U.S. Because of his work we had lived internationally and had no U.S. holdings. I had to look for a house in the States because each family member was living separately with friends, and we needed to be together. I had to go back to Australia to pack up our house there and ship everything back to the U.S. Some of it arrived damaged, and I had to deal with the insurance through Lloyd's of London. Not until months later did I have time to deal with grieving." Gladi B.

"Helping others helps me get through the grief. You never really get over it. You just cry until there are no more tears. It's not the first time in the world someone has lost a spouse. This will either happen to a husband or a wife, and you can't really tell how you will react." Ruby C.

"Time really will heal the pain. I definitely grieved. At first, I was just grateful to get through each day. It was hard, but it did become easier. I'm still caught off guard with grief, like when I see the men's department in a store or have a thought of him. Even putting air in the tires or seeing a glass of champagne can trigger the grief because we used to say to each other, 'You're the air in my tires' and 'You're the bubbles in my champagne.' Other things we'd say to each other can bring it on. I never imagined it would be so hard, but the waves of grief become further apart, and the good memories come in." Jolene M.

And a final thought:

"Grief does come in waves, but every year it gets easier. Just keep going. Even thirteen years later, I can still get choked up. It will happen the rest of your life." Kay P.

Ask yourself—

After reading the chapter "Grieving," what are some of my immediate thoughts?

_____

_____

_____

_____

_____

Do I feel I'm doing everything I can to work through my grief?

_____

_____

_____

_____

_____

What are some things I might try to help me through this period of grieving?

_____

_____

_____

_____

_____

Have others been affected by my grieving?

_____

_____

_____

_____

_____

If yes, who are they, and how have they been affected?

_____

_____

_____

_____

_____

What am I going to do to change that?

_____

_____

_____

_____

_____

Is there anything about the grieving process I could tell someone that might help her?

_____

_____

_____

_____

_____

What I want to remember from this chapter:

_____

_____

_____

_____

_____

CHAPTER 3
Love and Memories

They'll Always Be There Even If He Isn't

All my life I've believed that Love Is Too Strong To Die. It may sound simplistic, but believing this has helped me through the loss of family members, friends, and, most recently, the loss of my beloved husband, Pete.

I'm sure you know how even the most wonderful of husbands can sometimes do or say something that makes you think, *I can't believe he just did (or said) that.* When my girlfriends and I were together and one of our husbands would stretch our patience to the limit, I'd always say, "And we've got the good ones." We girls would roll our eyes and laugh, but we knew it was true. I was so fortunate to have been married to Pete for forty-four years, and now that he's gone, all those wonderful memories we shared still make me smile.

How do you keep Love alive when the person you've loved isn't? What works for me is talking to him: After all those years of talking to Pete, I'm not about to stop now. Once when we were eating dinner out, a casual (unmarried) friend strolled over to our table. After greeting us and exchanging the usual pleasantries, he said, "I've been watching you two, and you actually talk to each other. Not all married couples do that."

I have to admit it was rather unsettling knowing that someone had been closely observing us, but I began noticing that there really are many married couples who either sit silently across the table from one another or look down at their phones as if the other person isn't even there, something Pete and I never did. I want to shout at these couples, "Look at each other! Talk! You don't know how much time you have left to be together!"

There's no way I could stop talking to Pete just because he's not here physically. I talk to him while I'm at home, in the car, or on my daily walk, sharing things just like I had for all those years. It's as natural for me to do that now as it was when I could see him, not just feel him in my heart. Talking to Pete helps me feel connected to him, and it feels natural doing it.

Before I cancelled Pete's cell phone service, I made a tape recording of his voicemail greeting and also of the last voicemail message he left for me. Pete was in rehab in Florida when he mistakenly called the number for our Wisconsin landline phone instead of my cell, leaving a brief message. I was stunned when weeks later I heard it on the answering machine, and hearing him talking so naturally was a precious gift. I'll always have those tapes to play when I want to hear his voice, and that means the world to me.

There are all the photos of the two of us on the poster boards that were displayed at the two funerals, plus hundreds more in our many albums, and looking at the pictures of our life together brings back all the joy of our marriage, which was filled with love and fun. Pete is smiling in virtually all the pictures, and I think to myself, *This was one happy guy!*

How blessed we were to have had each other as long as we did. The love we shared sustains me and gives me strength to continue to live my life as Pete would have wanted.

Other women who have been widowed still feel that love as they've rebuilt their lives. They want to share the many ways they've kept those memories alive.

"Here's what I did. I had two stepchildren and made each a memory book about their dad. The books were not photo albums, more like scrapbooks. Doing this helped me as I collected Post-its and other little notes their dad had written, birthday cards the kids had given him, pictures of their dad from childhood to adulthood, a lock of hair he had kept from each of them. Each book was different, and making them helped me so much as I put together these wonderful memories." Debbi C.

"After he died, I talked to him a lot. I see him in my grandchildren, especially my grandson. I feel sad because he's not there sharing in their lives. When our daughter was married two years after he died, she wore a garter made from one of his ties, so it was like her dad was walking her down the aisle. She kept that garter and, at the reception, threw another one. I miss dinners out with him." Lila S.

"Allow people to talk about him and share memories. I had a unique situation where the man I was with for six years had been friends with my husband. We were able to share memories of things that happened over the years. Sixteen years later people still talk about my husband. If I have a problem, I'll talk to my husband and say, 'Okay. I need help here.' I talk to him because he knows the background of things. One day my former partner asked why I was sad, and I told him, 'Today would have been our fiftieth wedding anniversary.' He said that he missed him, too." Barb W.

"I talked to him a lot. I remember the good times and how we made it through the bad times. Even if I was entering another chapter of my life, he was still in the book." Bobbi V.

"I still talk to him all the time, and he answers me in my head." Angie O.

"I still wear my wedding ring and had his sized to fit me. I wear both on the ring finger of my left hand. I talk to him but express it through writing. I have a journal and write to him in it." Joyce B.

"I still talk to him all the time." Carole C.

"I'll talk to him occasionally now, like 'It's a good thing you're not here to see this!' I talk to him more when I go to the cemetery. I'll tell him news of what's going on because I look at the grave marker and associate that with him. But when I leave, that association is gone. It makes me feel good to know we always said we loved each other, always kissed good night." Joanne W.

"I talk to him. For instance, I'll say, 'Good morning' and 'Good night' to him. When I take out the recycling bag, which he used to do, I'll say, 'Where are you? You should be doing this!' I have all the cards he gave me. There are the memories of what was serious at the time, but now you laugh about them." Audrey C.

"I talked a lot to him in the beginning. When I go to his grave two or three times a year, I talk to him and say prayers." Nancy J.

"I talk to him all the time. I don't go to the cemetery. I want to remember the good times." Shirley W.

"Eight years later I still have his pictures out. I call my stepchildren on his birthday and on the anniversary of the day he passed. A friend of mine kept a journal after her husband passed, and I wish I had done that." Lee M.

"You decide to spend every day living life. You don't fill the hole in your heart, but you carry on. I think it's easier for women because we have to deal with everyday things, while men are concerned with work and business. In my head I ask, 'Why aren't you here with me?'" Kay J.

"It's wonderful to talk to him and share things with him. When I have the car races on TV, it feels like he's in his chair watching them." Carol L.

"That love never leaves. I talked to him all the time before I remarried." Kathy H.

"I use a walker, and if I fell, I'd be an invalid. I'm afraid of falling if it's slippery or raining. Seven or eight times I've been out, the sky is getting dark, and I'm getting close to home. I'll pray to him to get me home. When I get home before the roads get slippery, I'll thank him for protecting me." Mary B.

"I talk to both the husbands I've lost and tell each one 'good night' and that I love him." Gladi B.

"I'd talk to him, get mad at him for not being there when the challenges would come up. I recognize the love and respect we had and wish he were here to share things with." Pearl G.

"We had talked and joked about when one of us would die, what kind of car the other would buy. Death wasn't frightening to us. I talk to him sometimes but not as much now. We had worked so hard to buy our place in Florida, and he asked that his ashes be scattered there. That's what my family and I did. I read a poem and walked into the water at night and scattered his ashes and threw flowers." Kay P.

"I talk to him all the time sharing things." Jolene M.

"That connection is still there. I 'yell' at him all the time because a few days before his heart attack, he told a friend he wasn't feeling well but didn't tell me. He hadn't wanted to get new stainless steel appliances because he thought stainless steel was a fad. After he died, I replaced our kitchen appliances with stainless steel. I told him, "You might not like it, but that's what I'm doing.' I collect gnomes, and I can hear him thinking that I'm nuts, but I'm still doing it." Lyn L.

"I feel he's near me when, for no reason, the three-way lightbulb in the bedroom keeps turning on and off. I'll say, 'Keep turning that light on and off.'" Sandy G.

"I still say, 'Good morning' and 'Good night' to him." Joan A.

"Every time I pass the recliner he sat in, I feel sad. I still sit on my end of the sofa. I feel lucky to have had my two wonderful husbands. At times, I'll think, I'm not special. How could I be so lucky? A week ago I had his ashes interred in Arlington National Cemetery in Washington, D.C. It was an emotional ceremony and took me back to two years ago when he died. A good friend had interred her husband there and told me how to start the process, which took a long time. My husband had been in the Air Force and had been honored with the French Legion of Honor award. I thought Arlington would be a fitting tribute to him. I talk to my second husband when I'm on the expressway and ask him to keep me safe. I remember he would always say, 'Hurry back!' when I'd leave." Jan B.

"Honor his memory. Share stories about him with friends. Remember, no one is getting out of this life alive. I took the ribbons from the funeral flowers and made bookmarks from them. When I find one, it's like a hug. The day before he died, he took his golf glove off and put it in the side pocket of the car's passenger side. (I was doing the driving.) When I returned the lease car and was cleaning it out, I found his glove and now keep it in every car I buy." Beverly K.

"I mentally talk to him if I'm trying to fix something. I'll ask him, 'What would you do?' and the memories of what he taught me come back, and I'm able to fix it." Lou H.

"It is an adjustment (being without him), but what makes it easier for me is seeing so much of him in his children and grandchildren. He is missed tremendously as he was such a good man, husband, dad, grandfather, friend, and attorney." Sherry J.

"I keep asking him, 'Where are you?' I have his pictures around, and they make me both happy and sad." Karen C.

"When I walk in the door, I'll say, 'I'm home!'" Ruby C.

"His pictures are all around. I talk to him all the time. I kept his voicemail for two years so I could hear his voice." Ginny G.

"I still talk to both of the husbands I lost." Marijo Z.

"I say, 'Good morning' and 'Good night' to his picture." Judie N.

"My husband comes to me in vivid dreams, and I have to reach across the bed to see if he's there. I still talk to him. On what would have been our fiftieth wedding anniversary, I bought myself a beautiful bracelet. I went to the cemetery, sat down, and showed him what 'he' had given me for our anniversary. I don't go the cemetery as much as I used to. When I drive past the cemetery, I'll blow a kiss to him." Barb B.

And a final thought:

"I talk to him and feel him guiding me always. I thank him for the legacy he left me to enjoy every day. I thank him for the love we had and for our son." Evelyn C.

Ask yourself—

What were my immediate thoughts after reading this chapter "Love and Memories"?

_____

_____

_____

_____

Love and Memories

What are some special memories that bring me comfort?

_____

_____

_____

_____

_____

What are some routines we had that I can continue to make me feel close to my husband?

_____

_____

_____

_____

What advice could I give someone newly widowed about keeping those loving memories alive?

_____

_____

_____

_____

What I want to remember from this chapter:

_____

_____

_____

_____

CHAPTER 4
Signs

Are You Open to Signs That He's Still Watching Over You?

It's not a matter of having psychic ability like you read about or see on TV. It's being open to the idea that when your loved one passes over, he may find a way to let you know he's still with you; I've said before that I believe Love Is Too Strong To Die. I also believe if a husband is sending signs to tell you he's still watching over you, it would be very frustrating for him to have those signs ignored or passed off as coincidences.

Since Pete passed, I've had many signs that he's still in my life. Driving my car one afternoon, I asked Pete to send me one of those signs. I looked at the car in front of me, and the three letters after the numbers on the license plate were GLM, the same letters Pete had on his license plate. I've never seen those letters on a license plate before or since.

Here's another example. Sometimes Pete and I would be channel-surfing and find ourselves watching old *Leave*

It to Beaver reruns. The Beaver's brother Wally had a best friend who was nicknamed Lumpy, and there were times I'd tease Pete by calling him Lumpy. One Sunday morning as I entered our church's parking lot, I told Pete I was open to any signs that he wanted to send. Sure enough, there on the car in front of me was the personalized license plate "Lumpy"! I don't believe in coincidences. Pete loved cars, and it makes sense to me that he'd use license plates to communicate.

Still another example. Returning to our Florida condo the fall after Pete's passing, I set the alarm clock for 7:30 A.M. Not wanting to be awakened by the clock radio, I double-checked to make sure that the radio alarm button was turned off. The next morning I was awakened by Paul McCartney singing the refrain "I love you, I love you" from "Silly Love Songs." Since Pete and I would always begin every day by saying, "Good morning! Love you. Start the day!" that told me he was still with me no matter where I was.

When I'm on my daily walks, more often than not, I'm followed by white butterflies, so close to me that I can almost reach out and touch them. On my walk the day after Pete passed, a white cat with black markings appeared next to the trees along my route and followed me until it suddenly disappeared. I told my friends that if Pete wanted to get my attention, a cat was certainly the way to go about it.

After I returned to Wisconsin, our across-the-driveway neighbor Jim told me that on the day Pete passed in Florida, our solar-operated garage lights, which had automatically turned on every night before, remained dark that night. When Jim went to check on them the next day, the light switch inside the garage was on, so there was no conceivable reason for the lights to be off. Could Pete have sent another sign, this time a "goodbye" to the neighbors who loved him or to the home he loved so much? I like to think he had.

The most amazing sign that Pete is still watching over me occurred while I was writing this book. I developed a cold that caused me to cough throughout the night, and I was unable to sleep. Suddenly, I heard a voice clearly say, "Missin' ya." I automatically answered, "Missin' you, too, honey." At that same moment, the numbers on the digital clock next to the bed changed from 4:39 to 4:40, the exact time of Pete's passing.

I'm not the only one who has had signs from a deceased husband. Many of the following women who have been widowed have experienced their share of signs, as well.

"I remember one very specific thing that happened three years after my husband passed. I was at a famous archeological site in Ireland and could feel his arm around me. I cried because I actually felt it." Pearl G.

"After my husband passed, I could hear him telling me to 'move out of Wisconsin. The weather will get you.' I woke up at 3:00 A.M. and said, 'I'm moving out of Wisconsin!' I could hear him telling me to get the house sold. I moved to The Villages in Florida and have never regretted it. My arthritis is much better. Every so often I can smell him next to me in bed, and it makes me happy because I'm missing that connection to him." Angie O.

"I see his initials all the time on license plates, and so does my granddaughter." Kay P.

"I don't get them as much now. When I get vivid dreams about him, it's like he's there with me, and he's animated and talking to me." Barb B.

"Early on I'd get tingles, and my friend would call them '(my husband's name) Tingles.' Shooting stars were special to us. We'd sit on the dock at night and watch them. My puppy wanted to go out unusually early one morning. I took him outside and saw shooting stars. I feel a connection to my husband when I see eagles, which were also special to us. At the party after my husband's memorial service, a close friend asked his time of death. Our friend said he didn't know if he should tell me or not but he had had a dream in which there was a huge gate and a large gust of wind. He turned to his wife and said, 'I think (my husband's name) just died.' It was the exact day and time my husband had died. Our friend could not have known that, and I was so glad he told me." Joyce B.

"I feel his presence if I really think about it, more so when I'm missing him more than usual." Audrey C.

"A week after the funeral, I said to him, 'Please try to contact me. I'm open to signs.' I'm very close to my two granddaughters and went to Atlanta to visit them. Everyone was away, and I was at the house alone outside, crying. A big windstorm came up, and I grabbed cushions to take inside. Suddenly, I realized the only wind was near the evergreen close to where I'd been crying. There was absolutely no rustle of leaves on any other tree around me. Everything else around me was calm. I felt that the wind which was only around me was a sign telling me he had arrived in Heaven." Lee M.

"Oh, yes! The second night after he died, I was getting ready for bed and felt a hug. I knew it was him." Debbi C.

"I don't know if I have signs, but I know he's watching over me. Sometimes, early in the morning, I'll have a vivid dream where we're doing something together. Then I'll wake up, and I'll think, *Oh, darn!*" Kay J.

"Yes, I get signs mostly through music. When a song comes on that he liked, I'll say, 'I see you, honey.' We were boaters, and friends wanted to throw flowers into the water at a spot where he and I liked to sit and watch the sunset. There was no wind, and someone said the flowers would float back to shore. Just as they threw the flowers, the wind shifted and took the flowers out to sea. The sun was setting, and a boat exactly like ours went across the sunset. Another time I was in a store when one of his favorite Beach Boys songs, 'Kokomo,' came on. I suddenly saw an ornament made out of the same material as the shirt he was wearing at his memorial service,. Of course I bought the ornament." Barb W.

"Yes, I'm very comfortable that he's part of my life. It's very real and comforting to feel his presence." Carol L.

"I felt one of my deceased husbands come and lie down with me after he died. A clock I had bought with my other husband stopped working at the moment he died. The man who checked it said its insides were fine. He gave the pendulum a tap, and it began working. The time it had stopped was the exact time listed on my husband's death certificate. The phone lines went crazy for one week after he died." Marijo Z.

"Yes and no. I feel his presence in my condo. I have an artificial tree in my bedroom, and every once in a while the leaves will move. I'll ask, 'Is that you, honey?' When I hear a strange sound, I'll ask the same question." Mary B.

"I was outside on the lanai and heard my name being called softly." Joan A.

"I had a sense of peace and felt his energy when I was feeling down. There were vivid dreams that I still remember eleven years later. I feel that he's happy. When I met my future husband, I felt an overwhelming sense of approval from my husband who had passed." Bobbi V.

"I feel his presence when I see butterflies, angel figurines, feathers, animals, pennies, or bees, which he was allergic to. One morning I made coffee and walked out to the back porch. The ceiling fan turned on even though I had not hit the switch." Jolene M.

"I had a vivid dream that he was standing in the hallway smiling. It was so comforting." Karen C.

"One night I woke and saw the back of his head in bed next to me. I used to have a recurring dream in which he was telling me that he was in love with a dark-haired woman, which I'm not. It was devastating to me. My friend is a psychologist and told me the dream meant my husband was setting me free. A man cleaning the gutters informed me I needed a new roof, which I knew was going to be very expensive. Shortly after this, there was a huge hailstorm, and the roof was damaged. The insurance company paid for a new roof, and I always said that my husband had sent that hailstorm. We always say my husband sent my son-in-law for my daughter, who didn't get married until she was forty-two. They're so perfect together." Lila S.

"After he died, friends whom I had known since high school invited me to stay with them for a while. While I was there, I felt a wave of emotion come over me. I felt it was a message from him telling me everything was going to work out. I'll never forget that." Lyn L.

"Three days after he died, I looked at the paper, and the headline was 'Home and Free at Last!' Another day I was looking for a Bible verse to share with someone and turned to Romans 12:12—'Rejoicing in hope; patient in tribulation; continuing instant in prayer.'" Beverly K.

"My first husband was in the construction business, and it's easy to envision him standing in a field at a job. After he died, I heard him at the bottom of the stairs, saying my name. After my second husband died, I felt something like a touch on my shoulder." Jan B.

"The morning after he died, I was in bed waking up and felt a kiss on my cheek." Lou H.

"I had a dream about him but couldn't understand what he was saying to me. My horoscope that day read, 'Someone is trying to get in touch with you from far away.' His godchild had a vivid dream about him. She said he walked toward her and said how his legs, which had been swollen, were healthy again. She said he looked so happy and was smiling. That made me feel so comforted." Judie N.

"You have to be open to signs. I was lying in bed and saw him going from room to room. Another time I was in bed and felt him next to me. I felt the mattress, and there was an indentation that was warm. When I was on a cruise, I felt someone in my room. My husband was lying next to my bed and said, 'You're going to be okay.' I also find dimes in strange places." Kathy H.

"I'll find coins in strange places. I found a dime on the pickleball court. The night he passed, there were two dimes on the floor next to his bedside in the hospital." Sandy G.

"He guides me every day. I'll find bird feathers in times of crisis. When I'm in turmoil, I'll find a feather on the ground. Once I was driving and had a strong feeling to change roads. I took another route and, by doing that, avoided a four-car accident that I would have been right in the middle of. I'll get a feeling—*this isn't going to be good*—, like he's talking to me. I'll see cardinals in the yard that keep coming back. I believe he sent me my cat Mikey, who is inquisitive and kind just like my husband was. I feel his spirit is in Mikey. My friend had a psychic reading, and my husband came through and said he was proud of me." Evelyn C.

"After my first husband passed, I had a vivid dream in which I was standing on a pathway; people were carrying his casket ahead of me around a corner so I didn't bump into him. I looked down into the casket. He had his eyes closed, but he said, 'How about a dance, baby?' Both of us loved to dance, and that was so reassuring to me, like he was still talking to me." Gladi B.

"We were the third owners of our home, and it has a swimming pool. I needed to put the plunger in and stretched my arm as far as it would go, but it wouldn't reach far enough. I asked him for help, and, suddenly, I was able to reach it. That made me smile because I could feel him watching me." Ginny G.

And a final thought:

"One week after my husband passed, I could swear I felt him holding my hand when I was in bed. Then six months after he passed, I was lying on the couch and saw him standing in the kitchen. He looked young like he had when we were first married. He was healthy and had both his legs. (One had been amputated.). I was scared, and I cried. He was gone before I could get up to go to him. I'll never forget those two experiences." Nancy J.

Ask yourself—

What are some of my thoughts after reading this chapter "Signs That He's Still With You"?

_____

_____

_____

_____

_____

Am I open to any signs that my husband is watching over me?

_____

_____

_____

_____

_____

Have I had any signs since he passed?

_____

_____

_____

_____

_____

If I have had signs, how did they make me feel?

_____

_____

_____

_____

_____

What could I tell someone about possible signs that her husband is still watching over her?

_____

_____

_____

_____

_____

What I want to remember from this chapter:

_____

_____

_____

_____

_____

CHAPTER 5
Dealing with Regrets

Don't Obsess Over What
You Can't Change

This is the most difficult chapter introduction for me to write and, perhaps, for you to read. After our husbands have passed, if we think back to what we wish we did or didn't say or do, it causes us to have regrets and saddens us. It's one thing to know in your head that you were under stress, that so many things were happening simultaneously, that if you could do it over, you'd do it differently. It's another thing to keep dwelling upon something when you know there's nothing you can do to change it. I try to keep the Serenity Prayer in my mind. "God, grant me the serenity to accept the things I cannot change, the courage to change the things I can, and (what I think is the most important part) the wisdom to know the difference." If you're going to move on to a healthy widowhood, you need to let go of any regrets you may have. I know that it's easier said than done, but we can do it if we make the effort. It's all part of the healing.

I have no regrets about our marriage, which was a love affair. I used to tell Pete that he had more kisses and "I love you's" in one day than many husbands have in their entire lives. He'd give me that "Pete smile" and say, "You've got that right." We showed we loved one another through words and actions. Love, respect, fun, friendship, and trust were present every day. There will always be "Pete and Bonnie" stories for our friends and family to share.

However, I do have regrets about some things that occurred near the end. My first regret is that I didn't take our two cats, Riley and Murphy, to visit Pete in rehab when he kept telling me how much he missed them. Most cats don't like going to visit places the way dogs do. I thought taking them out of their home environment would be too disruptive and was afraid of creating additional turmoil in the midst of everything else that was going on. In hindsight, I could have gotten one of my girlfriends to help with the cats, the cats could have stayed in their carriers, and after Pete had seen them, my friend could have taken them back to the condo, leaving me to stay with Pete. I only thought of that solution much later after Pete was gone.

My second regret is that I didn't accept Pete was actively dying until the very end. You would think with my volunteering at AngelsGrace Hospice in Wisconsin for over nine years that I would have recognized the signs, but, as our doctor told me, it's different when it's your own loved one. Pete had rallied from a health crisis so many times in the past that I still thought he could come through this one. We called him the Energizer Bunny and said he had nine lives like his cats. That was my thinking as I sat next to his hospital bed and pleaded, "You've got to get well, sweetheart! I can't make it without you." He looked at me and very matter-of-factly said, "Yes, you can." I shared these regrets over lunch with my close friend Lyn, who told me, "Bonnie, those aren't that awful. You were there for Pete every day for all those years. Let those regrets go."

Lyn's right. We have to think about all the caring things we did for our husbands and the many words of love we shared with them; let the negative thoughts go. That's what our husbands would want us to do. I can just hear Pete saying in an unbelieving tone of voice, "You're upset about that?"

My advice is to be a friend to yourself, and tell yourself what you would tell a friend if they felt as you do. I'm also suggesting that you share your regrets with someone you trust like I did with Lyn. I felt so much better afterward. I've also thought about writing my regrets on balloons and releasing them to soar away into the sky.

Within this chapter, you'll learn that others who have been widowed have had regrets, and they offer advice for dealing with them, along with their stories.

"Give yourself permission to go on. You did the best you could at that time. You tried your best. If you had time before he passed like I did, you could touch and talk. It was both the gift and the pain of an extended illness." Pearl G.

"The past is the past. Try to put any regrets out of your mind. You can't fix it. We all have regrets at some point." Jan B.

"You have to get past the regrets, or you can't heal. If there's something you feel regretful about, 'tell' your husband, and get it off your chest. We all have regrets, but if his passing is sudden, there's no time to say anything." Barb W.

"You can't go back. If you have a regret that you didn't go somewhere together, find someone—a friend or a relative—and go there with her. It makes you feel good, and it's good for others." Kay P.

"First, figure out if you have valid regrets or misplaced guilt. If it's a valid regret, you may need professional help. Our biggest regret is that we couldn't save them." Bobbi V.

"My regret is that I wasn't more vocal in expressing my feelings towards him. I think it's because we were so confident in the love we had after sixty-four years together. That was a blessing." Kay J.

"You can't obsess over any regrets you have. I did that at first. Time helps with regrets. My regret was that I didn't start going to his doctor appointments with him sooner and listened to what the doctors were saying. Then I did go, and the doctors were open as to what we had to do. If I had gone sooner, I would have better understood the situation. But I know he wouldn't have listened to me anyhow. I also regret he wasn't there for his daughter's wedding." Lila S.

"You're only human. You did the best you could. One of my biggest regrets is that my husband wouldn't talk about his feelings. I thought we had more time." Beverly K.

"My advice, which someone gave to me, is to remember you did the best you could for as long as you could. My regret is about the last hours of his life when he seemed to be doing well. I would have stayed with him. We can't know God's plans. I believe when we have regrets that Satan is behind that. Think of how fast your marriage went. In no time at all, you'll be together forever." Joyce B.

"I have no regrets. You can't look back. You have to tell yourself you did all you could." Kathy H.

"If you and your husband lived a nice life, forget any regrets and move on. I have no regrets. We did what we wanted and knew where we stood. We had a wonderful life." Shirley W.

"It's better to think about good, happy things. I was there for my husband; I have no regrets. My sister-in-law's husband died, and she regretted that she hadn't told him she loved him." Ginny G.

"Everyone has regrets of some sort. I regret I didn't push him to go to the doctor sooner. My husband had the flu and said what could a doctor do? Then his breathing changed, and he developed pneumonia. When I start to feel bad, I think of the good times, and the kids and I talk about all the fun we had. He said he wanted to be buried with his wedding band. I really didn't want to do that and asked my son what I should do. He said I should do what his dad wanted, so I buried it with him. Then my other son was getting married and said he had wanted his dad's ring for his wedding band. I wished I had known." Nancy J.

"Put your regrets behind you. You can't change anything. Think of the good things. If you keep thinking of regrets, you'll be depressed all the time." Carol L.

"I've never been hung up on regrets. You can't change yesterday: it will always be what was. Even though we did a lot, I might wish we had spent more time doing things we enjoyed together. I have this saying on my refrigerator, 'Yesterday is a cancelled check. Tomorrow is a promissory note. Today is the only cash you have—so spend it wisely.'" Audrey C.

"I believe our deceased husbands know how we feel, what we wish we had done or said. You can't spend time regretting. When my husband was close to death, I wanted to tell him I loved him, but I felt self-conscious with the nurses and doctors in the room." Marijo Z.

"It was such a major effort trying to get him to live that I didn't realize he was dying. He wanted a family picture taken because he said it might be the last one. It was." Lou H.

"Why didn't I see he was sick? I have to live with that." Sandy G.

"Everyone who loses a loved one has regrets. There's always one more thing you want to say or do. Value what you did do for him. Value he left this world knowing he was loved. You don't have the power. God does. When my husband was ready to go into hospice, he asked me, 'What do you want me to do?' I couldn't answer him; it wasn't my question to answer. A priest told me not to regret not being with my husband when he died. The priest said a soul can't leave the body if a loved one is hovering over him. My husband chose when to go." Evelyn C.

"I have no regrets. Instead of questioning God about why things happened, I thank Him for all my blessings." Gladi B.

"You can't be everything. We're only human and not perfect." Carole C.

"I only have one regret because I took good care of my husband and kept him going longer than he would have without me. He fell on the floor and wouldn't let me call the EMTs. I couldn't get him up by myself and yelled at him. Then I cried and said I was so sorry. He told me that I shouldn't feel bad, that he understood. When you have regrets, you have to focus on the good things. You can't erase what happened; you have to own it. It won't go away. You have to realize it wasn't in your character." Lee M.

"Know that you did all you could and that some things are out of your hands. If it's their time, it's their time. God must have a plan." Lyn L.

"I remember what I did have, not what I don't have. I was lucky to have him in my life." Karen C.

"I don't have a lot of guilt or regrets. We shared our love. There are some small regrets like I shouldn't have gone out with my girlfriends every Wednesday." Jolene M.

"Things are never going to change, so you need to move forward. It's not easy. I pray to God for guidance. My husband died of a heart attack while I was out of state with a dying friend. Sometimes I think if I had been home, I could have gotten him to a doctor sooner. But our doctor said it wouldn't have made any difference. I believe God puts you where you belong, and that helps." Angie O.

"If you thought about all the regrets, you'd feel sad all the time, so you can't do that." Judie N.

"If you have regrets, you can't move on. What's one more dinner (you could have had) or one more 'I love you'? If you have a regret, like you didn't take a vacation while he was alive, then that wasn't the moment or time for it. You can't go on like that, regretting something." Debbi C.

"You can't change things; you have to go on." Ruby C.

"If you have regrets about something, remember that you probably did your best, and don't dwell on the regrets. You have to go on. Turn the regrets around, and remember the good things that mean more. The past is the past; move on. Maybe I wish we would have traveled more. I know I did what was right and what he would have wanted me to do." Barb B.

And a final thought:

"If you didn't verbalize that you loved him but knew he understood you did, then you should be fine. The regret is for you, but he knew. It's hindsight to say you would have done anything differently. Of all the topics, this one caused me the most concern, not because of how it would help someone else but how it helped me to think. My regret was that I didn't mouth off about things that upset me because I didn't want to rock the boat. Sixteen years ago when he died, I wasn't the person I am now. I was quiet. Now that I'm alone, I only have me to rely on. I'm a different person. Can't say I wish I would have spoken up because that wasn't the person I am now." Joanne W.

Ask yourself—

What are some of my thoughts after reading this chapter "Dealing with Regrets"?

_____

_____

_____

_____

_____

Do I have any regrets?

_____

_____

_____

_____

_____

If yes, what are they?

_____

_____

_____

_____

What are some ways I can put any regrets behind me and move on in my healing?

_____

_____

_____

_____

What advice would I give to someone who was dwelling on a regret she couldn't let go?

_____

_____

_____

_____

What I want to remember from this chapter:

_____

_____

_____

_____

_____

CHAPTER 6
Family Dynamics
Realize There May Be Changes

Since you've been widowed, you may find that family dynamics have shifted in response to your new status. Pete and I never had children, so my family now consists of my precious cats, Riley and Murphy, my two brothers and their wives, Pete's surviving brother and sister and their spouses, his late brother's widow, nephews, nieces, and cousins. I've been blessed with family members who are there to offer support and help when I need them. Yet, I've never felt "smothered" by relatives thinking they need to make up for Pete being gone by hovering over me.

Fortunately for me, my in-laws, Pete's brother Terry and his wife Marcia, lived near us in Florida during Pete's final hospitalizations and rehab and those last thirty-two hours of hospice. We gave one another strength and became closer as a result of everything we experienced together.

Three days before Pete entered hospice, our Florida car started to have major problems, and I needed to buy a different car, something I had never done without Pete, who loved cars and enjoyed shopping for them. When it was time for me to get a different car, he would go to dealerships and find a car he thought I would like. Then he'd take me to see it, and I was always delighted with the cars he chose for me. With Pete so desperately ill, this time it was Terry who went car shopping with me, and together we found my 2012 Honda CRV, which I loved as soon as I test-drove it. We were both sad at not being able to share the exciting news of my car purchase with Pete, who would have loved hearing about it but was now sleeping much of the time.

Less than four days later when Pete entered hospice, it was my sister-in-law Marcia who accompanied me on the initial visit to the funeral home where I made arrangements for Pete's Florida funeral. I'll never forget how my in-laws were there for me when I needed them the most.

When I flew back to Wisconsin after Pete passed, Terry and Marcia flew with me to help with the two cats. Upon our arrival, I wasn't alone as I walked into the house that no longer had Pete living there. I had been in Florida for the past seven months, the house had been vacant, and a lot of work needed to be done. In the days that followed, Terry and Marcia were such a help in getting the house, inside and out, set up for the reception at our home following the funeral. Terry and Marcia are not only my in-laws; they've become much-cherished friends.

My brother Greg lives in Wisconsin with his wife Debbi, and my brother Bill and his wife Ellen have a home in Tennessee. From the time Pete's health began to decline in

Florida until he passed in hospice, we were all communicating by phone almost every day. Debbi had lost a husband before she married Greg, and she gave me her support and understanding. As Pete's condition became critical, my brothers offered to fly down to Florida; I told them that wasn't necessary because I had Terry and Marcia with me, and I would need my family's help after I returned home.

That proved to be the case when Greg and Debbi arrived at the Wisconsin house in their white pickup truck loaded with canopies, lawn ornaments, plants, tables, chairs, and coolers. They took charge of setting up everything for the luncheon at our home following the next day's funeral. Bill and Ellen drove up from Nashville to offer their support, and it was beyond comforting to have my family and their love surrounding me.

I'm delighted that my great-niece Kayla and I have become close now that she's in Wisconsin and not her home state of Minnesota. Kayla is a college student at the University of Wisconsin-Milwaukee, about forty-five minutes from my home. During the summer after Pete passed, Kayla took a chemistry course at a college near me. She would often drive out to my home before class to have dinner, study, and watch our favorite TV shows; sometimes she even spent the night. Kayla may not have realized it, but her fun-filled, youthful companionship not only brought me great joy; it helped me transition to my new life without Pete.

The love of my family has sustained me since I lost Pete, and I can't imagine what I would have done without it. However, families are made up of individuals who sometimes react differently to changes and losses within their family circle.

Learning how other women who have been widowed have dealt with family issues that arose may be a big help in dealing with those you encounter. At the very least, as you read their stories, you'll know you're not alone in what you're experiencing.

"My husband told his children to take care of me. I had to explain to them that he didn't mean for them to hover over me. I carry on traditions we had, but I've had to set up boundaries. Now, we go out to eat after church instead of going to my house. My stepchildren are outspoken. They had to sign for their names to be taken off the trust for my house and warned me that I might meet a 'creep' who would take the house. I said, 'Give me some credit. I'm not stupid.' A cousin of my husband's actually told me, 'It's time to take off the mourning clothes and reengage with life.' I've learned I couldn't be both grandmother and grandfather to my grandchildren. I have to do what is best for me. My granddaughter brought me flowers and cookies on the anniversary of her grandfather's death." Joyce B.

"My children became more protective. They helped me move back to Wisconsin from Florida." Bobbi V.

"All family members handle the loss of a loved one differently. Some move towards you, and some move away.

You need to understand everyone has their own level on how they feel about death. My husband's brother and his mom were distant and handled it in their own way. Our son didn't want to accept it. He was angry at his dad, who was also his best friend, for leaving him. He's not over the grief and has not gotten through the grieving process. Our son goes nonstop; he can't stop long enough to feel the (healing) pain." Evelyn C.

"No issues there. I lost five close family members in five years." Beverly K.

"My sons hear their dad's voice and talk to him all the time. They're good husbands and fathers. When my husband passed, there was only one sister left from his family. She told me I was her last connection to a family member. We're close, and she comes to visit me. I enjoy her and tell her I'm thankful to be included in her family's events." Angie O.

"My brothers and their wives were in New York, so I had limited support from family, but I knew they were there if I needed them. My concern was for my teenage son. He was very quiet and wouldn't talk about his feelings. He didn't handle losing his dad very well, and it was hard to get through to him. But we came through it." Joanne W.

"Holidays are different. My children have picked up hosting the holidays." Lila S.

"My sons hover over me. One son calls every day at 4:30 P.M. on the button. They come to see me and are so protective of me. They don't want me driving to their homes, so they come to get me. They do let me make my own decisions, and I have my own freedom." Mary B.

"My brother-in-law did not come to his brother's funeral. He said he knew his brother was going to die, as if no one else had known. He and I don't speak at all. My grief counselor said, 'The link in the chain is broken. When your husband died, the chain broke.' My sons were twenty-five, twenty-seven, and twenty-nine. My middle son moved back in with me for two weeks. It hurt me to see them lose their dad, and I still get teary when I think of that." Kathy H.

"My husband's family can still be upsetting after thirty years. One of his sons is very good to me, but my stepdaughter is not friendly. It isn't like I married him after a divorce. We had both lost our spouses and had known one another before. My husband often said if it wasn't for me, he 'would have been gone long ago.' I think it's a sad situation, and he would be very unhappy about it." Jan B.

"My family didn't want me to be alone, so they'd take turns staying with me." Kay P.

"One of my in-laws was a mean and nasty person who had been estranged from us. My brother told her to come to the funeral home before the service, and she was to have no contact with me. I was so worried that she'd cause a scene because she loved drama. She didn't arrive early. When my friends saw her coming through the reception line, three sons of my friends stood like bodyguards around me and were very protective. She wasn't in my husband's will and wanted to see a copy of it, which she had no right to see. My brother wrote up a document that said she had to stay away from me." Barb W.

"In the beginning, my kids called to check on me. I had always taught them to be independent. I was their example of an independent woman—I was a pilot, and an RN. If I needed help, I would ask for it." Audrey C.

"Friends can be the family you choose who will help you to get through it. I've been on my own since I was nineteen. My mother died when I was ten, and my father was hospitalized from the time I was sixteen. Both of my parents were only children, and my sister lived away." Barb B.

"I had no changes within the family. We all still are close and get together." Shirley W.

"My daughter stayed with me for a while. My former son-in-law helped me with things, and he still calls me every day. My brother-in-law, my husband's twin, said I was still young and had his permission to remarry. He told me, 'We are your family now.' Two years after my husband died, my daughter said I had a 'sad face' and went online to the eHarmony dating site. She showed me a profile of a guy from our church. I laughed and said, 'Not interested.'" Ginny G.

"My in-laws were fabulous and called me to see how I was doing. There were seven children in my husband's family, and now only two are alive. He always said as time went on, we'd all be together. His younger brother and his father both died at forty-nine years on the same date and at the same time. My kids were good. They stopped or called every day to see if I needed anything." Nancy J.

"The first couple of years after he died were okay with my step-kids. Once I remarried, I wasn't included in as many things with them." Debbi C.

"We've always been close. We celebrated holidays and family events together. That's not changed. I've talked to my son more because he's handling my financial things. My daughter handles the taxes. Since my husband passed, our family has been together every Christmas except one, when my son spent it with his dying mother-in-law. The grandchildren grow up and move on." Kay J.

"My youngest son calls almost every day. My daughter is a take-charge person. If I ask her for something, she'll get it done. They know I'm very independent." Carol L.

"My eleven-year-old daughter, who died in the train accident with her father, shared a birthday with her sister. My daughter says her birthday is not the same. My children act like they lost religion. My brother-in-law and his wife really helped me." Marijo Z.

"My daughter and I bought a house and live together. My brother-in-law and nephews are very helpful." Lou H.

"After my husband died, his children resented the fact that I might get some of his money. My stepdaughter has been nicer to me lately ever since I had a wedding shower for my grandson. I took two of my granddaughters to Paris and took another one to Portland, Oregon, where she learned to surf. We traveled with one of my friends and her daughter and had a great time." Lee M.

"I found in the months following the sudden passing of my first husband, the father of my four children, how important it was to the family that I remain as strong and positive as they were trying to be. We always tried to remember wonderful memories we had with him. Each child had to adjust to living in the U.S. again, in a new home and school or university and under new circumstances. I am so thankful my husband and I were blessed with wonderful children who really helped me on this uncharted journey then and now as they continue to show their love to me." Gladi B.

"My family was very supportive. My youngest son works from home and came home to be with me." Sandy G.

"I'm not really close to many of his family members, but we weren't close before he died." Lyn L.

"I couldn't have come through this without my daughters. Sometimes they do try to act like my parents." Karen C.

"There was always too much drama with the in-laws. I put up with it when he alive. Now that he's gone, I can't be bothered with them." Ruby C.

"I have very supportive daughters. Sometimes my wonderful daughters try to parent me." Joan A.

"Most family members were sensitive to my loss and would let me talk if I wanted to talk. My brother-in-law lived out of state and saw more of us when we were all in Florida. He wasn't with me for the initial grieving process, and when I saw him in Florida, he wanted me to grieve with him. I had to tell him he was bringing me down, that I couldn't continue to grow if I remained grieving." Joleen M.

And a final thought:

"At different times family members will take on different roles. Each of my children took on a role after their father died. One worried, one enabled and said, 'Don't worry about what people think. Do what you want to do.' At times, another almost took on the role of a husband in being responsible for me. He said I didn't have to read a book on budgeting because I was already doing it. He also wanted me to go to a bereavement class at the hospice. Two of my three children didn't want me to sell the house, but when I did, they didn't question my choice." Pearl G.

Ask yourself—

What are my immediate thoughts after reading the chapter "Family Dynamics"?

_____

_____

_____

_____

_____

Have relationships within my family changed since my husband passed?

_____

_____

_____

_____

If yes, what changes did I notice?

_____

_____

_____

_____

Was I surprised by any of these changes or did I expect them?

_____

_____

_____

_____

_____

How have I dealt with any changes that have occurred?

_____

_____

_____

_____

_____

What is the healthiest way for me to deal with any changes in the future?

_____

_____

_____

_____

_____

What I want to remember from this chapter:

_____

_____

_____

_____

_____

CHAPTER 7
Dealing with Others' Concern

When in Doubt, a Simple
"Thank You" Will Suffice

As soon as people learn you've lost your husband, you'll get a variety of reactions. The most common is, "Oh, I'm so sorry." This may or may not be accompanied by a head-tilt and a sad, somewhat forlorn look. I'm sure the person means well, but it's a little disconcerting the first few times you're on the receiving end of this response, because so many people do it unconsciously. If it's someone you know, they may ask what happened, and it's up to you as to how much you feel like sharing. There will be times when you want to keep the explanation short, and other times you'll want to share more details. Never feel that you're obligated to tell anyone more than you feel comfortable with at any particular time.

Early on in my widowhood, I found that it was very easy to get choked up when friends expressed sympathy, or I was asked about my loss; even when I believed I had gotten my emotions under control, I found they were closer to the surface than I had realized. As stated in the chapter title, you can keep any exchange short with a simple "Thank you" or "Thank you for your concern." If the person doing the asking is a casual acquaintance or a stranger at a get-together, for example, I always keep it short. I'm not about to get into an intense conversation about the loss of my husband with someone I barely know. Pete's illness and passing are too personal for that.

The people who are most aware of what you're going through are other widows, and you'll find them compassionate and, usually, not inclined to press you for too many details. Even a widow who has remarried is reminded of her feelings after she lost her husband and will often tell you that things will get better with time. She's been there and wants to give reassurance that you'll get through this. At least, that's been my experience.

Women who have been widowed have their own ways of dealing with the condolence issue.

"My advice is to express your feelings. Talk if you want. People want to share your loss. They might be afraid you'll break down if they ask how you're doing. Talking about your loss makes it harder but also easier. Does that make sense? I was in shock at the funeral. I decided to go with my feelings and just be myself." Lou H.

"When people ask about my husband, I do tell them but not in complete details." Mary B.

"Just say 'thank you.' If you want to talk, fine. If not, be upfront and say, 'I don't want to talk about it.' There's a nosy lady in my neighborhood who fishes for information. When I see her approaching, I walk away." Lyn L.

"'Thank you' is always a good answer. Someone I didn't recognize told me how much he enjoyed being with my husband. I just said, 'Thank you. He enjoyed being with you, too.' I'm proud of my husband. Sometimes women who lose their husbands want to share all the details. Let them talk even though you may feel awkward." Kay J.

"A 'thank you' will cover most expressions of sympathy from others. I sent thank-you notes to everyone who came. There were some people whom I expected to show up who didn't." Barb B.

"'Thank you. I appreciate your thoughts' is always good to say. It was so heart-wrenching and touching to read the cards people sent. It was very cathartic. It was also very touching when people asked if I would like a mass card, and, of course, I said, 'Yes.'" Audrey C.

"Some new widows may not be ready to deal with answering questions, and that's okay. I would say thank you and give people the whole story if they asked. I thought my answering could help others." Bobbi V.

"'Thank you' is good to say. New people I meet don't know about my loss, so I don't have to talk about it." Jan B.

"The people who are hardest to deal with are the ones who say, 'I wouldn't be able to exist without my husband!' or 'How do you deal with it? You're smiling.' These people don't know at all and think if they emphasize with you, you'll feel better. But they're going home with their husband, and you're alone. Some would say, 'If you have no children, how are you getting through this?' I'd say, 'I never had children, so I never had to depend on them. I've always had to be independent.' If people asked what happened because he died out of state, I'd explain briefly that he was on the heart transplant list and had a heart attack." Barb W.

"I'd say, 'Thank you for caring.' People don't really know what to say. I didn't want to dwell on details." Debbi C.

"I would tell anyone who asked what had happened. If you wanted, you could say, 'I really don't want to talk about it.' Someone asked me about my finances, and I said, 'We spent all our money traveling.'" Lee M.

"I'd say, 'We're all going to die someday. I knew this was coming, so I started grieving before, but thank you for your concern.'" Kay P.

"Accept their concern. Most people mean well. At my husband's wake, a woman I've known since high school went on and on about her unruly grandchildren. It was like she was using my husband's wake as a social event. She never once expressed sympathy to me on the loss of my husband. I was in a state of shock at her behavior. I've never spoken to her since." Lila S.

"You can share a certain amount of information if you wish. If the person is being intrusive, say, 'I don't care to talk about this. It's still very tender for me.' If it gets to be too much, say, 'Enough about this. Let's talk about you.'" Beverly K.

"You can say, 'I appreciate your thoughts.' You can change the subject. I didn't encourage people to talk about their relative who had died from the same disease that took my husband." Pearl G.

"'Thank you for your concern' is what I would say." Judie N.

"I never went into a big discussion about his death. If they weren't good friends, instead of being serious, I'd act upbeat about it. I had a hard time verbalizing my loss. The exception was when I broke the news of his death to our longtime friends and bridge partners. I said, 'Well, we're going to have to get a new fourth for bridge.' I can't believe I did that." Joanne W.

"When they offer their condolences, they bring up their own losses. Let others talk about their losses. It's the only way for them to get over it." Angie O.

"If it's people you don't know well, 'Thank you. I appreciate it' is enough. There's a difference between sympathy and empathy. When people show you sympathy, they'll come alongside you, maybe touch or pat your arm. Empathy is from people who know what you're going through. The longer you go through the grieving process, the more you can tell the difference between the two. Two and a half years later, people still ask, 'How are you doing?' There's no good way to answer that. If they haven't been there, they won't know that. I hate it when someone says, 'I lost my husband.' I didn't 'lose' mine. I know exactly where he is." Joyce B.

"People don't realize what they're saying. You don't have to give any lengthy explanations. 'Thank you' is always a good response." Carol L.

"Do what makes you feel comfortable. It doesn't bother me when people ask for details about his passing. It makes me feel good to talk about him." Shirley W.

"I would just say, 'Thank you.' If they asked what he died of, I would say matter-of-factly, 'Brain cancer.' I hated it when people said they were sorry for my loss. It sounded like I lost my shoe or something. When someone would say about me, 'She's a widow,' I didn't like it because that doesn't define who you are. They don't say about other women, 'She's a divorcée,' 'She's married,' or 'She's single.'" Kathy H.

"If someone asks about my husband, I'll say, 'Thank you.' If they ask what he was like, I'll say, 'He had a great sense of humor.'" Ginny G.

"People say really stupid things to you after your loss. One man came into our liquor store after my husband died and said, 'You have to get back on the horse!' I didn't give him a response because I knew he said stupid things. A woman said to me, 'My cat died, and I know how you feel.' I didn't respond." Marijo Z.

"I just say thank you." Sandy G.

"Say thank you and walk away. Only someone who has experienced the loss of a spouse will get it. Widows who are in a new relationship don't remember what it was like after they lost their husband. You don't owe anyone anything. Don't feel pressure that you have to appease others. Give no details. 'What did you do with his ashes?' deserves no answer. Say, 'I don't care to answer that,' and walk away." Evelyn C.

"After my second husband died, a man started stopping and knocking on my door. He was asking very personal questions, and I said, 'That's very personal, and I don't want to talk about it.'" Gladi B.

"I always just said, 'Thank you. I appreciate it.'" Carole C.

"Most people don't ask me about him." Karen C.

"When a casual acquaintance asked me what had happened, I asked a friend standing there to handle it for me. She said, 'Jolene is having a hard time.'" Jolene M.

"If they ask what he died from, I say, 'A-fib. Thank you for your concern.'" Joan A.

And a final thought:

"Looking back when I was at his funeral, it was like I was dreaming, not believing he was gone. I was sad but not crushed. I knew it was his time. He always said, 'Death is a happiness. You go to a better place, and life is beautiful.

There's no pain or trouble.' It didn't bother me to explain to people at the funeral what had happened, that he had the flu, which went into pneumonia; he went to the doctor; he came home, I called the EMTs, but they couldn't do anything. Seeing people at the funeral who loved him helped me." Nancy J.

Ask yourself—

What are my thoughts after reading this chapter "Dealing with Others' Concern"?

_____

_____

_____

_____

What was my outward response when people offered their condolences?

_____

_____

_____

_____

_____

How did these expressions of sympathy make me feel inside?

_____

_____

_____

_____

_____

Did this chapter change the way I'll offer condolences to others in the future? If so, how?

_____

_____

_____

_____

_____

What I want to remember from this chapter:

_____

_____

_____

_____

_____

CHAPTER 8
Choosing How You'll Live Your Life
You Have More Power Than You Realize

When I taught high school English, I would tell my freshman students they had more power than they realized. They could choose to make good choices, which would have positive consequences, or they could make poor choices, which would lead to negative consequences. I was talking to them with regard to choices in friends, study habits, classroom behavior, anything that might come up in this new, somewhat scary world of high school they were entering.

The reason I'm mentioning this is that making good choices also applies to those of us who have entered the somewhat scary world of widowhood. We can choose to make good choices that will lead to positive outcomes, or experience the negative consequences that will arise from poor choices we've chosen to make. We have the power to choose the type of life we want to live now that we're women who have become widowed.

We need to realize when we make a choice, that choice can be compared to a stone thrown into a lake. The stone lands in the water and sends out ripples from that spot. The choices we make send out ripples that not only affect us, but also the people around us. We have suffered a great loss; that hole in our heart may grow smaller over time, but I've been told it never completely heals. We need to accept this and choose to move on. If we don't, we're like a car spinning its wheels, staying in one place and never moving out of it to continue on its journey. I'm not saying you'll never have those times when your loss comes crashing down on you. I am saying all of us need to realize that everyone has difficulties and losses in life. We need to remember we're not the only ones.

You have a choice to make as to how you're going to live the rest of your life. Are you going to choose unhappiness and retreat within yourself, closing yourself off from new adventures and new opportunities? If this is your choice, how do you think the people you come into contact with are going to respond to you? Remember what I said about those ripples radiating out from your choices. Would you want to be around someone who never smiles, who acts unhappy all the time, who causes others to feel depressed? I wouldn't, and I don't think you would, either. People want to be around someone who makes them feel good, who cares about what is going on in their lives, who gives off positive energy, a person who has risen out of a dark place and has chosen happiness over unhappiness.

Yes, moving on takes strength, but you've been strong before when you needed to be. Sometimes people will say to you, "Your husband would want you to be happy." I don't know about your husband, but my husband Pete would be the first to say to me, "Be happy! We had a wonderful forty-four years together, and you were a great wife! If you feel me around you as you say you do, then get on with your life and know I'm cheering you on!" Remember, the choices you make will have an effect on your healing progress.

These women who have been widowed share how they moved on with their lives after losing the men they loved.

"Give yourself permission to make choices. The surprising thing is now you can make all the choices; you can eat when you want, watch TV when you want. It's so different because when you're married, you don't realize how connected you are to the needs and wishes of your husband. Now you can think of your own needs." Beverly K.

"It's like alternately swimming and treading water to reach a shore in the distance. Forevermore, you'll have to swim to that shore. The waves will get high, and you'll have to tread water, but keep swimming. You don't know where on shore you'll land, but you have to have faith. God has a plan for you, so keep swimming to shore." Barb W.

"Your experience isn't like anyone else's—similar maybe, but we are all unique. Time will heal. The first couple of mornings it was hard to get out of bed. Then I thought coffee might taste good, which was a step in my healing process. Another step was remodeling rooms in my house, investing in my future. My husband wouldn't want me to be sad. I'm young, and he was always happy and would want me to be happy, too, and move on with my life. I've always been a positive person, and I believe a person's attitude continues after a loss. I was in a place where I needed to feel joy. Even though you're grieving, you're forced to do things, and time is passing. I was not mindful; my thoughts were scattered, and I realized I was zoning out at times when I was driving or at the house. I handled it by keeping checklists on paper or in my head. For example, *Did I turn the iron or burner off? Do I have my keys?* I'd see a new bruise and not remember hitting something. My husband fought in Vietnam and always told me that the most dangerous time is the last leg (of a patrol) or, for me, when I'm getting close to home if I'm driving. I remembered his words, and chose to be mindful of what I was doing." Jolene M.

"My husband and I always said, 'Life goes on.' You can't sit in the house and feel sorry for yourself. You're here, and he's not. It's the way it is, and you have to do things that make you happy." Lyn L.

"I have my family and friends. I chose to enjoy my life." Shirley W.

"You need to keep striving for a life with purpose. My first husband was only forty-four years old when he passed, but I was determined to be the loving, caring, positive person that he was and that he would have wanted me to be. While he was in college in Minnesota, I had taught school there but would have had to be recertified to teach in

Michigan, where my family and I were now living following his passing. The president of a large bank offered me a job in Financial Services which I really enjoyed for eighteen years. It was truly a blessing for me. I became involved with people and worked with the United Way, various senior citizen groups, and many other charities, which was not only fulfilling to me but enabled me to give back to those less fortunate." Gladi B.

"After my husband died, I knew I had to go on for the sake of my sons. You tell yourself today is another day. You do what you have to do. You can get a job or volunteer. There's no way I'd just sit in a chair not doing anything. I couldn't do that to my children. I love dogs and decided to become a dog sitter, boarding the dogs in my home. I had a business card made, and people call me to take care of their dogs." Angie O.

"You had a good marriage, and now he's gone. You want to have good life memories. If you have a career or job, you can focus on that. I had good memories and a good marriage. I was young and wanted companionship. There was a woman who lost her husband a month after I lost mine. She didn't want to move on and felt so sorry for herself. She didn't lead a healthy lifestyle. I didn't want to be like her." Debbi C.

"I'm basically an optimist. You need to look at everything as an opportunity. When you're married, you have to take your husband's wishes into consideration. For example, *Which earrings should I wear?* Now it's just what you want.

When you lose a friend—and at my age it happens—try to make a new one. It's important to do anything you can to enlarge your life. Too many people have unrealistic expectations of things coming their way without any effort on their part." Audrey C.

"You have the choice to live life as your husband would want you to. If your husband truly loved you, he would want you to be happy. You have to realize you're making choices for yourself, not you and your husband. It's almost a sense of independence or liberation." Bobbi V.

"You have to get involved with people. Find things to do. I volunteer but don't want to do it on a regular basis." Barb B.

"My husband died before tax time, and there were a lot of things that needed to be done. I have more power now because I didn't have to do as much before." Kay P.

"I chose to live my life and be happy. I was able to come back to our place in Florida. I chose to travel with my girlfriends and cousins. There are many widows, ten out of twelve women, in my golf group in Illinois." Lila S.

"I chose to go away to a favorite place of ours on the Mississippi River. It was a quiet time for me while I made some decisions." Pearl G.

"You just do it. I had my teenage son to think of. It was now strictly up to me to make sure he studied so he'd get through high school, up to me to make sure he stayed out of trouble." Joanne W.

"You've been dealt the cards. You can play them negatively or positively. My grief counselor said, 'Put on your happy face because people don't want to be around someone who is sad all the time.' I was trying to juggle all the balls in the air for the sake of my sons. I had so many changes at once—I retired, lost my husband, stepped down from a position on a board I'd been serving on. I tried to keep appearing like I was okay and put on a happy face because I didn't want the kids to worry. I was by myself but not lonely." Kathy H.

"I took each day as it came after my husband passed. Taking care of the pool, which he had done, was therapy for me. I chose to live each day the way my husband would want me to. Live each day." Ginny G.

"I wanted to stay alive and go on for the children and his memory. You don't think about how you'll go on right away. There's so much to do. A friend asked if I would like to work for her at her business a couple of days a week, that she had so much work and needed help. So on Tuesdays and Thursdays, I help with filing, typing, sorting bills. I really enjoy it." Nancy J.

"I chose to continue with the schedule we always had, to not totally change things. We had a good life. I needed the same structure, the same friends. When you're alone at night or in the house, you've got to have something you enjoy doing. When I have nothing planned, I'll do quilting or embroidery or read a book. You don't have to be out and about every day, but have one thing in the future, like in the next three to four days, to look forward to. Another thing I choose to do is to have the TV on so it's not so quiet." Kay J.

"We were very happy. My home is my comfort zone, and I feel his presence." Carol L.

"It was an unconscious choice for me to go on. I just did it. I had to carry on the best I could. It was a terrible time for our business, and I had to deal with the banks and lawyers. People weren't always honest or looking out for my best interests." Lou H.

"It's been a year and a half, and I still feel overwhelmed. There are times I choose to pull back and be by myself." Sandy G.

"Do what makes you feel comfortable. Don't think about it. I had no choice but to go on. I had to keep the business going because I had four children to support. It was the right thing to do, to go on with life. I felt better being with people." Marijo Z.

"My choice was to keep to my routine." Joan A.

"I chose to keep my faith and to continue the good relationship I have with my sons. I'm very independent and say, 'I can do it myself.' I prayed I would continue to be independent and make good decisions. I made the choice to have fun. My husband and I would go to the casino every once in a while. After he died, I went with a friend, and I won! I won't make a habit of it or bet more than I can afford to lose. I know when to quit." Mary B.

"Now I'm more positive and stronger. I get tired of people saying how strong I am. I don't always feel like that inside." Karen C.

"I'm still in the house we built in Florida. For me to begin a new chapter in my life, I need a new environment, so I'm going to sell the house. I think it will be better for me when I get my own place. The house I'm in now is too much work. I'm still trying to figure out what would make me happiest." Lee M.

"Take it one day at a time. Put one foot in front of the other. Everything will fall into place. You have no choice but to move on. Women are brave." Ruby C.

"I go to the recreation center to play cards and take line dancing lessons. It's nice to meet new people. I do go out to eat. I feel uncomfortable sitting in a booth by myself, so even though I don't drink, I'll sit at the bar to eat. I've met nice people to visit with while I've been there. When my first husband died, I was only fifty-three. My husband hadn't wanted me to work while the kids were young, so I had no social security, and it would be a long time before I could receive his. I didn't know what I was going to do, but I took a job. After my second husband and I started dating, we built a twin single-family home to be my security and rented out half of it. My mother was living with us and wanted my full attention. She was resentful when I'd spend time with my husband, who was ill. She died shortly before he did." Jan B.

"Choose each day to be grateful for what you have. Get out of bed when you're ready; there's no stopwatch. Losing him brought me to my knees. I wish I had been kinder to myself. There's a hollow hole in your heart that can't be filled, and I still have my moments. You can move on, but you can't feel joy while that piece of you is gone. You realize you're no longer thinking for two but for one." Evelyn C.

And a final thought:

"Whatever you need to do to get through life, that's what you do. Always keep in mind this life is not all there is. I've chosen to help other people, and I'm going to train my dog to be a therapy dog and take her to visit cancer patients. People told me my husband would be so proud of me. I'm not unhappy, but I don't have the level of happiness I had before losing him. I have a deeper appreciation for things in life now. I used to be a 'people pleaser' but no longer. I don't need drama or negativity in my life. I realize how short life is and feel an urgency to have quality in my life." Joyce B.

Ask yourself—

What were my immediate thoughts after reading this chapter "Choosing How You'll Live Your Life"?

_____

_____

_____

_____

_____

What are my motivations in choosing to live my life to its fullest?

_____

_____

_____

_____

_____

How am I going to live the fullest, most productive life I can?

_____

_____

_____

_____

_____

This is what I'd tell a new widow if she asked my advice about moving on without her husband:

_____

_____

_____

_____

_____

What I want to remember from this chapter:

_____

_____

_____

_____

_____

CHAPTER 9
Taking Care of Yourself

No One Is There to Catch You If You Fall!

It's important to remind you that *you* are responsible for your well-being, and that means you need to be proactive in taking care of your health and safety. There's no husband at home to take care of you when you don't feel well or to help you if you fall. You're on your own now, and it's smart to take care of yourself in a variety of ways.

To stay as healthy as possible, I try to walk two miles every day, do a half hour of stretching daily, use the weight-resistance machines at the gym three days a week, and dance whenever I get the chance, even if it's at home by myself with just my two cats watching. If I didn't keep to this exercise regimen, the pain from my lifelong scoliosis would flare up and keep me from doing much of anything, and I'm too social to stay at home. Yes, exercise is insurance that my bones and joints stay strong, but the biggest benefit is to my mental health. I'm proud of myself after I exercise and feel confident that what I'm doing is contributing to a healthy body now and in the future.

I understand not everyone is able to do everything I'm doing, but most everyone can do something. If you have exercised in the past, you need to keep it up. This is no time to slack off on healthy habits. If you haven't exercised before, the first step is, of course, to check with your doctor and ask what type of exercise would be best for you. You can walk, take exercise classes—including those specifically for seniors—use exercise bands or light weights, even exercise while sitting in a chair. These are just a few options to getting and staying physically fit no matter how old you are and if your physical condition permits it.

Your doctor should be eager to offer suggestions and happy that you're interested in doing something to improve your physical well-being. If you're not currently taking vitamin supplements, ask your doctor if they would be beneficial. Eating well is important, too, and we'll discuss that at length in another chapter. If you feel you could be eating healthier, your doctor can recommend a nutrition class or nutritionist. Our doctor recommended that Pete and I take a nutrition class at the hospital after Pete was diagnosed with congestive heart failure. We found it extremely informative.

If your current doctor doesn't appear enthused about your interest in exercising or eating nutritionally, ask friends or family to recommend another doctor who will help you. It's your health, and you need to take control in becoming the healthiest you can be. That includes regular doctor checkups and diagnostic tests to keep ahead of any health problems that may arise.

Earlier in this introduction I mentioned the danger of falling. Since most falls happen inside the home, here's something you can do to lessen the risk of that happening. Before you get out of bed during the night or in the morning, sit on the edge of the bed and allow yourself a few moments before standing. Why? Pausing before getting up allows your body to adjust after lying flat. Taking time to regain your equilibrium can definitely aid in preventing a fall.

Another consideration with regard to your well-being is to eliminate unsafe conditions around your home that could cause you to have an accident. Invest in a sturdy stepladder. No more using that wobbly stool or chair that happens to be handy. I did that while trying to fix a towel rack in the bathroom. The small dressing table chair I chose to stand on fell over, and I went with it. I had a hard landing on the floor and bruises to show for my stupidity. Obviously, I could have been badly hurt, but I was lucky and learned a valuable lesson (and bought that sturdy stepladder!).

Here are some other safety suggestions I think are important. Buy an inexpensive reaching tool with rubber grips on the end. Be sure any scatter or area rugs have non-slip backings, or buy rubber backings to put under the rugs to keep them in place. Safety grab bars and a non-slip surface to stand on are must-haves in the tub or shower. I prefer a teak shower mat, which provides a good surface to stand on, is easy to clean, and doesn't get moldy; you can buy it at Bed Bath & Beyond using one of their coupons. Have a peephole installed in your door so you know who's outside. If you live in a house, you can install outside motion-detector lights. No, I don't expect you to install the grab bars, peephole, or outside lights yourself, unless you're really handy at doing those projects. If you're not handy (and I'm not), one option is to ask friends or family to recommend (here's your criteria) a capable, honest, reliable, reasonably priced, licensed, insured handyman who will be able to do repairs and improvements around the house. I located my handyman from reviews on our neighborhood website. He has repaired many things inside and outside my home, and I don't have to keep asking relatives or friends for help.

Women who have been widowed have developed various ways of taking care of themselves and are eager to share their suggestions with you.

"I was a nurse, so this is important to me. Exercise, get fresh air, eat wholesome food, talk to people every day, get involved. If friends are housebound, get on the phone and talk to them or visit." Audrey C.

"I try to be careful in whatever I'm doing." Karen C.

"Engage your brain all the time so you don't hurt yourself. Don't make sudden moves, try not to hurry when you're doing things, slow down. When the driveway iced up, I had it taken care of so I wouldn't fall. If I don't feel well, I'll get in to the doctor. I used to have my mom to go to for a remedy, but she's gone. Now I can't access her wisdom. You can always call a friend for advice before you go to a doctor.

Listen to your body. Watch your diet. Listen to your doctor. I had to change my diet to avoid Type 2 diabetes, and doing that brought my A1C count down. I got mad at the dietician who said I needed meds and changed my diet to 'show her'. It worked—no meds!" Joanne W.

"Live healthy, laugh, socialize! I always had to make a list, sort of like a journal, of what I needed to do." Debbi C.

"Eat healthy, exercise as much as possible. I've always taken care of myself physically. I walk more. If it's hot outside, I'll walk in a mall or in a store." Jan B.

"My daughter calls me every morning to check on me." Joan A.

"I'm much more proactive. I pay the bills as they come in. I fill the gas tank when it's down to a third. Take care of your health. I enjoy walking, but if the weather is bad, I'll use my exercise bike. You can walk the aisles at the grocery store instead of just running in to buy something. Watch your alcohol intake. I drink more water when I'm out socially because I'm driving. Make sure the doors are locked before you go to bed. I keep a pole in the patio doorframe." Pearl G.

"Follow your doctor's recommendations for tests and procedures like colonoscopies. Take any meds ordered. I sold the house and now live in a condo with double locks. I'm my grandchildren's last living grandparent, and I want to be around for them—and for me, too! I have safety bars in the showers. I chose a car repair within walking distance to my condo, but they still want to drive me home while the car is being fixed. You have to fight for things. I had just bought a new car, and the remote key broke. When I took it back to the dealership, the repair guy said I'd have to pay for a new key. I didn't accept that and went to the salesman who sold me the car. He said the dealership would cover the new key." Lila S.

"My advice is to be kind to yourself. No guilt and don't try to suppress emotion." Jolene M.

"Before I remarried, if I was going to be on a ladder, I'd do it five minutes before someone was coming over. Then if I fell, someone would be there to find me. After I heard a noise in the middle of the night, I installed an alarm system. I have a fabulous handyman who charges $25.00 an hour and says to call him when I get a list of ten things for him to do. I top off my gas tank when it gets to the halfway mark. I walk every day before bedtime. You have to do something every day to get you away from being inside. I did water aerobics every day at 10:30." Kathy H.

"I don't do anything special. Just be careful." Ruby C.

"Try to keep things as normal as possible in your new normal. There's great peace in routine. Start establishing your own routine. If you exercised before, keep exercising. You can walk or bike. If you don't like to exercise, don't. Make a pot of tea or coffee, read a paper or a book. Once I was past the initial busy time, I either ate bad food or didn't eat at all. I ate a lot of microwave popcorn. Neighbors would smell it and ask, 'Is that all you eat?' Some people eat the wrong food because they feel they're entitled to do that due to their tragedy. If it helps during the first few months, do it. After that, you need to be disciplined and eat nourishing food." Barb W.

"I live with my daughter, and I can maintain our home myself. We have a light on the patio and are talking about getting a security camera, but we're concerned about Internet hackers watching. A mechanic friend gives me advice if I'm having car problems, and then I'll take the car to the dealership. I have a man who'll pick up the lawnmower and snowblower if they need work. I'll go to the chiropractor if I need to. I also try to work out on the resistance machines and treadmill at the YMCA because I have health issues—fibromyalgia, Hashimoto's disease, and sleep apnea—so sometimes I'm limited as to what I'm able to do." Lou H.

"Get a sturdy stepladder. Be aware of your surroundings. Don't leave your purse in the grocery cart. Take your time doing things. When you go down the stairs, hold on to the banister. Get a motion light outside. Get an extra lock. Place a mat in the tub so you don't slip." Sandy G.

"Go to the doctor when you need to. I fell, and it's taking a long time for me to heal. Since I fell, I make sure there's nothing in the halls or near doorways to cause me to trip and fall. I have a safety bar in the tub. I use the railing on the stairs. A friend gave my husband a chairlift for the basement stairs so he could get down there to work on his hobbies. I use that when I need to go down to the basement." Nancy J.

"I always take my phone with me outside when I go to get the mail ever since I had my accident. I had gone to get the mail, stepped outside, and my new doormats were slippery. I caught my ankle on the cement steps and broke it. I managed to crawl back to the house, and called 911. Now I call my friend in the morning, or she'll call me. Have some contact with someone. Establish a safety routine: you'll call at a certain time or the other person will." Lyn L.

"Early on after he died, I tended to gloss over taking care of myself, didn't do as much as I should have. As time passed, I took better care of myself. My older son lives with me, so I have someone there." Carole C.

"I take a bone density test because my doctor wanted me to do that. I exercise and walk each day. I fell in the bedroom, hit my head, and didn't go to the doctor right away. Four weeks later my right side began to get weak, and I had trouble saying words. Finally, I went to the doctor, who said I had a brain hematoma and had to go to the hospital. He said I was lucky I hadn't had a seizure or stroke. Be careful, especially going down stairs." Ginny G.

"If you take care of yourself, you won't develop health issues. I've gone back to exercising. If I get sick, there's no one to take care of me. When I did get sick, I asked my daughter to take me to urgent care and asked a friend to get me Gatorade. I never was sick when I was taking care of my husband. For protection when I'm out, my daughter gave me a kitty keychain. The cat's ears are sharp and pointy; it's really a weapon." Joyce B.

"Prevention and safety should be the top concerns for everyone. I've started using a walker because it gives me more stability. I wear a GPS medical alert that tracks wherever I am and is not very expensive. I can wear it on my wrist or around my neck. It alerts someone if I fall, and it doesn't need satellites. My friend thought she didn't need assistance and didn't wear her alert. She left her walker in the car, fell in the house, and broke four ribs and her wrist. She lay helpless in her home for two days before her daughter found her. When I turned eighty-three, I decided no more driving back and forth between Wisconsin and Florida; it was time to draw the line. The time comes when you have to rethink things you used to do independently. You can always call Uber if you need to go somewhere. I checked out the company Comfort Keepers. Its employees are students, retirees, people who want part-time work and will do any job within reason. The company is registered in Wisconsin and Florida, where I need their services. They'll take you to the doctor, grocery shopping, and will even use your own car. I interviewed a lady employed there who took me to and from the doctor and then swept my garage. They charge $23.00 an hour with a four-hour minimum and are available twenty-four hours. It's my backup if I need someone. It's very comforting to have them and keeps me independent." Carol L.

"I have security for my condo. My sons had a camera installed, and I can look on my iPad and see who's at the door or at the computer room window. There are locks on the doors and high-impact glass on the windows, so they can't break easily. I have a safety chair and grips in the shower and a chair with arm handles in front of the bathroom counter. My neighbors watch me like a hawk!" Mary B.

"Call someone or have them call you every day. A Life Alert necklace is good to wear. Have a motion-detector light installed outside. If you can take care of it, you can always get a dog." Marijo Z.

"I wear a Guardian medical alert necklace. It transfers from one state to another. I tell the company when I'm leaving the state, when I'm on the plane, and when I arrive at my destination. They have that address. I have a lockbox on my door, and the Guardian company has the code to open the door if there's an emergency. It's very important that your medical alert can be transferred from one state to another." Gladi B.

"Your balance isn't as good as you get older. You need to slow down and use the railing as you go slowly down the stairs. Don't rush. You have all day to do things." Kay P.

"I worry about being alone. I could choke, and no one would know until I didn't show up for my friends' Thursday get-together. I don't go out swimming at night anymore. If you travel, get rid of your large suitcase and get a medium suitcase. The medium size is easier for you to lift, and you won't hurt your back. When my cousin came to visit, I had him take all the things in the house off the top shelves so I don't have to use the ladder to reach them. I had thick scatter rugs, which were easy for me to get tangled in, and changed to smoother rugs. I have Mace spray in the car and near my bed. I drive to Ohio and back. The car I had was getting up in mileage, and I traded it in for a more dependable car." Lee M.

"My widowed fifty-eight-year-old daughter lives with me, so I'm not alone. Just live each day." Shirley W.

"I walk, exercise, and there are many exercise classes at The Villages, where I live. I don't smoke or drink except for an occasional glass of wine. I try to do everything possible to stay upright. I ride my bike but not as much as I did before, because if I fall, I'm in trouble. You need to keep up with your doctor, dentist, and eye appointments. Talk to your doctor about increasing bone strength. I use a good stepstool but don't use a big ladder. In The Villages we have a privately owned community service, and the EMTs can be at your home in four minutes." Angie O.

"I had seven surgeries since my husband died, and I followed all my therapy instructions. I exercise but not as much as I should. Never miss your doctor appointments." Kay P.

"My advice is to make wise decisions. For example, I don't drive long distances anymore. I'm capable of it, but it's not wise to do it. I drive into my garage and stay in the car until the garage door closes behind me. Keep up with good car maintenance. Get a good handyman. Be careful of people trying to take advantage of widows." Beverly K.

"Surround yourself with people who fuel you, because you're running on empty. You're unable to fuel anyone because you don't have it. Do what gave you joy together. It's a gift to do that. Find something that gives you pleasure, like reading. Play cards, bridge, if you like. Take part in sports if you can. You need fun in your life. I'm glad I didn't give up golf. After a burglary, I had a computer pad installed on the door to replace the lock. I'm the only one who has the code. The pad comes with a handle and lock. Have a list of go-to people like mechanics, financial people, a handyman you can trust." Evelyn C.

And a final thought:

"Keep fit mentally and physically. You can do crossword puzzles, read, keep up on world events. I began an exercise program with my husband when he was in rehab. My doctor suggested yoga when I had leg problems, and it helped. I did Weight Watchers and now I'm a life member and don't have to pay. My exercise class added brain exercises and balance exercises. There's also chair yoga and chair boxing. Be safe. Don't go to shopping centers at night. I have a friend who calls me every night to make sure I'm safe. If I'm going out, I'll tell her. I called her when I fell off the stepladder and hit my head on the kitchen counter. She came over and drove me to the ER, where I had five stitches." Barb B.

Ask yourself—

What are my thoughts after reading this chapter "Taking Care of Yourself"?

_____

_____

_____

_____

_____

Were there any suggestions that really resonated with me?

_____

_____

_____

_____

How am I going to take better care of myself in the future?

_____

_____

_____

_____

What advice would I give another woman with regard to taking care of herself?

_____

_____

_____

_____

_____

What I want to remember from this chapter:

_____

_____

_____

_____

_____

CHAPTER 10
Pets in Your New Life

Never Underestimate the Power of a Purr

If you're already a pet owner, you know how much comfort your pet has brought you since you've become a widow. If you don't own a pet, but in the past you've thought about adopting one, now may be the time. Since Pete passed, our two cats, Riley and Murphy, have not only brought me comfort, but also love, companionship, entertainment, and so much more.

Pete and I always had cats throughout our forty-four years of marriage; I had four cats when we met, and the only time we were without a cat was during the summer of 2016 when we were traveling from our condo in Ft. Myers to Moffitt Cancer Center in Tampa for Pete's MDS (myelodysplastic syndrome) clinical trial. Our most recent cat, gentle eighteen-year-old Mickey, had passed away from cancer in May, and we didn't feel it was fair to bring a new feline into the family when we wouldn't be able to give him quality time during his adjustment period.

When we dropped out of the clinical trial in August and made plans to return to Wisconsin, I checked our local shelter's website and was drawn to the photo of an adorable six-month-old ginger kitten that was up for adoption. Long story short, as soon as we were back in Wisconsin, we adopted our sweet Riley. Riley was a perfect addition to our family and returned to Florida with us in the fall. He flew back with us to Wisconsin for Christmas, and when we returned to Florida after the holidays, it was with Riley and his new cat brother Murphy, a playful eight-month-old gray tabby from the same shelter. The boys bonded immediately, and we always said it was a match made in Heaven.

Riley and Murphy brought so much joy to Pete while he was home, and when Pete was hospitalized or in rehab, he loved hearing Riley and Murphy stories. I never returned home to an empty house after spending all day with Pete; my boys were always there to greet me, play, and sleep with me at night.

After Pete passed, the cats were definitely grieving with me and needed that extra love and attention that only their "mom" could provide, especially Riley, who had been Pete's cat. They filled any extra time I had, and I never felt alone. At night with a cat purring or sleeping on either side of me, the bed didn't feel as empty as it would have without them.

As I stated earlier, if you were without a pet while your husband was alive but wanted one, now that you're a widow, a pet will not only provide you with love and emotional support; you won't *feel* alone because you won't *be* alone. You'll have your pet, who needs you to take care of him or her and who will give you something else to think about besides yourself. Check the local humane societies and their websites, and consider older pets. Kittens and puppies are cute but will require more training. Ask the shelter workers or volunteers who help socialize the animals about any animal you're interested in adopting. These dedicated people interact with the animals on a daily basis and can give real insight into their temperament. You'll be rescuing an animal who needs a home, and I guarantee that animal will be rescuing you from sadness and loneliness, as well.

If you're unable to have a pet for whatever reason, you can still have that connection to an animal by volunteering to socialize animals at your local shelter or at an organization that provides support animals to those in need. You could also pet-sit for pets of your family or friends.

As you read what women who have been widowed say about pet ownership, you'll find many different points of view and various things for you to consider before adopting a pet.

"My cat Mikey is my lifesaver. He was a tiny stray kitten, and my friend Mary told me I had to take him, that he wouldn't make it if I didn't. I took him home, and he's such a joy for me. It's as if my husband sent him. I'm not alone; I have Mikey. We rescued each other and have a good life. I love him." Evelyn C.

"After my husband died, my doctor suggested I get a dog. I bought a Havanese puppy four months after losing my husband. My blood pressure has dropped twenty points since then. I find myself staying home because I don't want to leave her. She makes me so happy." Judie N.

"I used to have pets, but I'm done with that." Joan A.

"I love pets and used to have a dog and a cat. I'll get another cat and dog when I don't travel anymore and get my new place. I don't want to put them in a kennel if I go away. I miss having pets because you have something living to touch and are not alone." Lee M.

"I could write a book about how my cats and my dog have helped me since losing my husband. I'm not lonely with them around. Life would be sterile without them." Carole C.

"I used to have dogs. I'd love another, but what would I do with a dog when I want to travel? I get too attached to pets." Lyn L.

"Having a pet is a lifetime commitment. Don't rush into getting a pet unless you've wanted one before. You're going to have to take care of a pet. My cats were such a comfort to me after my husband died. They would cuddle and sleep with me. I slept in his T-shirt, and they could smell his scent on it. When I'd be crying, one of my cats would sit on the edge of the bed near me." Bobbi V.

"We used to have two dogs. I thought about getting another one, but I don't need a pet right now." Sandy G.

"When my husband passed, we had three dogs. One had been 'his' dog and then became mine. I had something to come home to. They gave me affection and unconditional love." Debbi C.

"We always had big dogs, golden retrievers, but they smelled. My daughter wants us to get another dog. We're looking for a smaller dog like a goldendoodle that doesn't smell so we can keep it inside." Lou H.

"My niece moved in with me for two years and brought her cat. She was gone a lot working and being with her fiancé, so her cat and I became close. I was surprised at how attached I became to that cat. I've been thinking of fostering a cat for an animal shelter." Lila S.

"I don't want a pet now. We had a dog named Katie, a little Boston terrier. She died a year after my husband. I remember thinking if something happened to me, Katie wouldn't have anyone. It can be very costly to take care of an older pet." Carol L.

"If you're lonely, you can always get a small dog." Marijo Z.

"I love dogs. If I didn't have my family around me, I'd get a dog for company. But then you have to take the dog outside even if the weather is bad or the ground is slippery. If I'd be out with my children, I'd have to go home to take care of the dog. A pet makes it hard to travel. It makes things more difficult. I'd definitely have to weigh the pros and cons of getting a pet." Kay J.

"I had my cat Petunia for fifteen years. She was a Siamese, and when my husband passed, she was so affectionate, which can be unusual for that breed. She would snuggle in bed with me, and I could tell she missed him. Having her was comforting and gave me someone to talk to." Barb B.

"I couldn't do it without my black goldendoodle, Jasper. I got him at six and a half months, and he's fourteen now. When you have a pet, you don't come home to an empty house. I dog-sit in my home, and the dogs have to meet Jasper and get along with him before I'll agree to take them. Ninety percent of my neighbors have dogs. It's amazing who you meet when you're walking your pet. When Jasper passes, I'll get another dog." Angie O.

"No, I don't have a pet now. We had a dog, and I can't put another dog to sleep. I love animals, but I want to be able to travel." Nancy J.

"My daughter who lives with me would like a dog, and maybe one day we'll get one. Right now, we dog-sit for my grandchildren's two dogs." Shirley W.

"I have Haley, our rescue cat. My husband chose her name. She sat with him day and night, so much so that I had to take her to her food. When he passed, Haley would paw at his clothes closet door. She would get inside and try to take his shirt down to lie on, or she'd lie on his shoes. She would sit at one end of the lanai staring in one direction for hours. The vet said she was looking for my husband. She sleeps with me and lies on his pillow, other times at the foot of the bed. I can talk to her about him. She's such a comfort to me. I'd be lost without her." Mary B.

"We had our dog for fourteen years. I wouldn't want another because I like to travel and don't want to board a dog or saddle someone else with the responsibility of taking care of it if I'm not at home." Joanne W.

"I don't have any pets. After my husband died, my son brought over his sweet pit bull to stay with me. I heard a strange noise in the middle of the night and had to wake up the dog, who was sleeping soundly on my bed. I told my son to take his dog back home. If someone would come over, that pit bull would lie down and roll over for a tummy rub." Kathy H.

"I'm a dog person and would enjoy the companionship. However, it wouldn't be fair to leave a dog home alone when I'm away volunteering for eight hours, plus drive time, and not be there to let it out. I'll pet every dog I see when I'm walking." Pearl G.

"I travel a lot, so it wouldn't be good to have a pet." Kay P.

"I don't have a pet now. My kids say I should get a dog or cat, but if I want to go somewhere, that would tie me down. My neighbor got a puppy. He loves her, but he needs a training class. I told her a pet is like a child except it has four feet." Jan B.

"Pets are absolutely important. I'm thinking of fostering kittens for a shelter when I get back to New York. I always had cats. It's important to do anything you can do to enlarge your life, but too many people have unrealistic expectations about pets." Audrey C.

"We lost our precious dog Bubby before my husband passed. We hadn't replaced him, which turned out to be a good thing for me because it's harder for one person to have a dog when working. I missed that unconditional love that a pet gives, so now I dog-sit for close friends and have an arsenal of pets. The dogs stay overnight; I walk them and play with them. I'm helping my friends, and the dogs are giving me love, comfort, and companionship." Jolene M.

And a final thought—

"I highly recommend a pet. You get unconditional love from animals. If you can't have or don't want a pet in your home, you can volunteer at a shelter or a place where they train dogs to be therapy dogs for vets and need volunteers to help socialize the dogs. I adopted my puppy Ellie and then adopted my kitten Echo for Ellie—and for me. Before I adopted my puppy, I would 'borrow' friends' dogs to walk. Pets are wonderful, and my pets make me laugh. My cat will sit on my shoulder. Pets are furry for a reason. Their fur absorbs tears." Joyce B.

Ask yourself—

What are some of my immediate thoughts after reading this chapter "Pets in Your New Life"?

_____

_____

_____

_____

_____

If I don't have a pet, what are some things I need to consider before getting one?

_____

_____

_____

_____

If I'm unable to have a pet in my home, what are some options for me to experience a connection with animals?

_____

_____

_____

_____

If I do have a pet, what qualities has my pet brought into my life?

_____

_____

_____

_____

_____

What advice would I give someone who is considering getting a pet?

_____

_____

_____

_____

_____

What I want to remember from this chapter:

_____

_____

_____

_____

_____

CHAPTER 11
The Year of "Firsts"

Time Goes On, and You Can, Too

Many people cautioned me that when the "first" of anything arrived—the first anniversary, the first birthday, the first Thanksgiving or Christmas without Pete—it was going to be very difficult. I made up my mind that since nothing was going to stop all these "firsts" from occurring, I would make them special and not spend them alone and in mourning, something Pete would have hated for me to do.

Pete passed on May 15, 2018, a little over a month after our April 13th forty-fourth wedding anniversary, which we celebrated in the dining room of the rehab facility at Table 13. We had a lovely dinner, great conversation, and a relaxing after-dinner "date" in the rehab courtyard surrounded by palm trees, colorful flowers, and birds chirping as they flew in and out of the bird feeders. That special day will always be a memory to treasure. Of course there was no way of knowing that Pete was in his final rally before everything crashed on May 1st, the day he was scheduled to return home.

In Wisconsin for the first Fourth of July without Pete, I drove to the home of my brother Greg and his wife Debbi. After dinner, we watched the fireworks sparkling over the lake from their pontoon boat as we had done so often with Pete. We talked about all the fun times we had had together and made sure to call brother Bill in Nashville to wish him happy birthday. It was comforting to be celebrating the holiday with Greg and Debbi on this first Fourth of July with Pete noticeably absent from our family circle.

For the first Thanksgiving without Pete, I was in Florida and spent the day with my in-laws, Terry and Marcia. Friends of theirs, whom Pete and I had met before, joined us for dinner, and it was nice to be with people who had known Pete and remembered the fun times.

Pete's birthday is December 20th, and for the first birthday he would be celebrating in Heaven, I had close friends of ours over for dinner, after which we gave a toast to Pete and sang "Happy Birthday." It was something he would have loved, and we all agreed that we could feel him smiling down on us. The tiny lights on my decorated Christmas palm tree twinkled in the corner of the living room, and I was glad I had listened to Pete the previous year and added those lights to accent the miniature ornaments already on the tree. Instead of sitting alone on this day, I surrounded myself with loving friends.

Suddenly, it was the first Christmas Eve in forty-four years without Pete by my side. Before heading to 9:00 Mass at St. John XXIII, I attended a small house party at my neighbors' condo. We had many laughs and a good time visiting, but in the midst of this holiday gathering made up of those who had known Pete, I began to feel that Christmas Eve was going to be more difficult for me than the other firsts.

I drove to church early because I knew Mass would be crowded, and when I arrived, the choir was singing traditional Christmas hymns as people entered. Sitting alone in the pew, I was flooded with memories of past Christmas Eves spent with Pete. When the choir sang the poignant "Mary, Did You Know?" my eyes filled with tears while I fought to gain control of my emotions. The Mass began, and as it commenced, the familiar words brought peace to my heart.

After Mass as we began to leave, the choir burst into a magnificent rendition of Handel's "Hallelujah Chorus"! I immediately stopped to listen. Pete had always loved this glorious song and maintained it wasn't really Christmas Eve until we had heard it, either in church or on TV after we returned home. Hearing the joyful words of praise took away much of my sadness and made me feel as if Pete had joined me for Christmas Eve, after all.

On Christmas Day I had dinner with three other couples at the home of dear friends. Two of the men were part of Pete's golfing foursome and reminisced about all the fun times they had had together. We stood in a circle with our hands joined as our host Gene said a beautiful and heartfelt prayer before dinner, ending with the feeling that Pete was right there with us. Surrounded by love, there was no room for sadness on this special day.

My first birthday without Pete arrived on January 13th, which was on a Sunday. I went to church in the morning and at the end of Mass received a special birthday blessing in the front of the church with my fellow January 13th birthday celebrants. At home, I propped the beautiful "To My Wife" card Pete had given me on my last birthday on the kitchen counter. I had a lovely lunch with my friend Gladi, visited with another friend Barb and her husband Rich (one of Pete's golf foursome), took a quick walk, and had dinner with my friend Peggy and her husband Craig. Friends and family called all day with birthday greetings, which made it a special day filled with love. I missed Pete so much on this first birthday in forty-six years without him, but I still felt him nearby.

Then it was February, and on the kitchen counter where I could easily see them, I placed the beautiful Valentine's Day cards Pete had given me for the past two years. Rereading them with the little comments he had written made me smile and treasure the love they represented. The next day I had dinner with close friends, which was very comforting, as well.

St. Patrick's Day was always special to Pete and me. We'd get together with a group of fun-loving friends to celebrate and always had the best time. On this first St. Patrick's Day without Pete, I had our close friends Dick and Karen staying with me during that time, so I wasn't alone. I had attended my friend Sandy's birthday party the day before, and she had sent me home with containers of food from the wonderful Burmese buffet we had all enjoyed. I had more than enough leftovers for Dick, Karen, and me, and we joked about the delicious Burmese meal replacing the traditional corned beef and cabbage. There's little time to feel nostalgic when you're surrounded by love and laughter.

In late March, my cousin Marilyn's beautiful, vivacious, thirty-seven-year-old daughter Amber tragically took her life after battling depression for many years. I flew from Florida to Wisconsin for her memorial service held on April 13th, the day Pete and I would have celebrated our forty-fifth wedding anniversary. This was also the wedding anniversary of two of my cousins, Amber's aunt Joan and uncle Gary. Instead of joyfully celebrating our anniversaries, family members comforted one another as we tried to come to terms with our family's devastating loss. There was no way I could have imagined spending that first wedding anniversary without Pete at Amber's memorial service. The unfailing love of family members and close friends sustained all of us on that sad day.

I began my first Easter Day without Pete by attending Mass at our church in Florida. The message of the Mass was that Easter is a time of hope, happiness, and the promise of everlasting life, a message that gave me such comfort. At the end of Mass, the choir sang Handel's "Hallelujah Chorus," which came as a wonderful surprise. Earlier I mentioned how I felt Pete's presence when the church choir sang that song on Christmas Eve. I felt that same connection to him upon hearing it again unexpectedly on Easter Sunday, the first time I've ever heard it sung on that day. The afternoon was spent with my in-laws, Terry and Marcia, and their friends who had known Pete. It was truly a blessed Easter Day.

There were other smaller firsts that were just as significant as the bigger events. There was the first time I ordered address labels printed with just my name and the first time I sent out our annual photo Christmas card without the two of us on it, just the cats and I. There was the first time I went to the grocery store and didn't buy food that Pete liked but I didn't. There will be other firsts that I haven't even considered yet, but I'll move on and hold all those years of love and fun memories close within my heart.

Women who have been widowed have various ways of dealing with their "year of firsts" and want to share them in the hope of making it easier for you.

"Think of others instead of yourself. Think positively. I focus on my children. I told them not to come down for Christmas, to have their own Christmas, that it was crucial for them to make their own traditions in their own homes. I didn't feel sorry for myself. Focus on those who care about you; don't focus on those who don't." Gladi B.

"My daughter hates Christmas because of our losses. That first Christmas I was busy working because I had no choice. We had to get through the holidays. Don't ignore the firsts even if they're hard to get through. It's good to be around children. Plan something on those first occasions or holidays. Don't sit alone. I sang in the choir; it was the only way I could go to church. Be with people you love or who care about you." Marijo Z.

"I suggest you continue with the way you did things before. I'm with my family at Christmas. On the first birthday without him, I felt bummed out and wanted to stay home. Last Easter I went to a different church where I didn't know everyone. That way I wouldn't see couples I know together, wouldn't be asked how I was doing." Kay J.

"The first year is hard. On Christmas my children came over. We talked about all the fun things we had done with their stepfather. I could hear his voice. Being with family and friends helped. The number one thing to do is to trust in God to get you through it." Ginny G.

"His birthday is hard. I say to him, 'Damn. You should be here.' I spent Christmas Eve with my family at their homes, and it was hard not having it at my house like we used to. On Christmas Day I had the neighbors over for pot roast. Having people around made it easier. It's good to be included in others' activities. People want you around if you're smiling." Angie O.

"Christmas morning was hard. Time really does help, and it's gotten easier. Now, on Christmas I recall all the wonderful times. I try to keep busy, and I go to church. On my husband's birthday my son posts pictures of his dad on Facebook. Eight years after my husband died, when my daughter got married, it was an emotionally mixed day; it was both a happy and a sad day for me." Lila S.

"I celebrated some firsts that year, but I couldn't celebrate New Year's Eve because that was so special to us. There's always time for reflection, and I have wonderful memories. After twenty years I hear a song or think of something, and I'm grateful I can recall those memories." Debbi C.

"Gird your loins and realize it's going to be hard. You'll think back and remember every other event when he was there. You'll think of the last time. Sometimes looking back might make you feel angry because he's not there with you. I celebrate his Heavenly Birthday." Bobbi V.

"Having my grandchildren with me for all the firsts made it easier because kids are so much fun to have around. Having family around at Thanksgiving helped me." Kay P.

"I don't know if you can make it easier. Keep busy, pray, stay positive. Read literature on grieving. All the feelings you're having are feelings others have gone through. It's good to celebrate the memories you had together. My widowed friend and I shared the same wedding anniversary, and we went out together. On the first anniversary of his death, what was to have been a small get-together became a large gathering of friends who shared memories and stories of him. The second year is also hard. It's not like the first. You need to be aware that some loneliness will creep in. Others go on with their lives, but your husband isn't there." Beverly K.

"I was taking my grieving class around the time of our first anniversary. A man in the class was whining about what his kids hadn't done for him. I told him he had to take responsibility for planning something. I go into a funk around his birthday. On the anniversary of his death, I'll go shopping or to a movie. On Valentine's Day I'll also go to a movie or lunch. Early on after he passed, I went to a movie alone and saw a group of people from church, and I was okay with being alone. I'll go to a grandchild's sporting event alone and talk to those sitting around me. I plan and don't mind doing things by myself. If I go out to eat alone, I'll take a book. Staring at someone else's table makes me feel sad. If I eat dinner at home, and if I'm not going out, I'll have wine. My husband's birthday is coming up. I'll spend it volunteering and then stop for dinner." Pearl G.

"If your husband had a long illness, be happy he's 'healthy' now." Ruby C.

"You can't get away from having that first year. For me, it was easier not to be with people because they'd bring him up and say, 'Oh, this is the first (whatever) without him.' Once they verbalized it, I felt bad. You can't not celebrate those events. Nothing will make it easier because someone will bring it up. It's human nature. People want you to know they're thinking of him, and so they mention it. Others may get emotional and then it's easier for you to cry. Others' sympathy makes it hard." Joanne W.

"Don't be too hard on yourself. You'll cry. Establish your own traditions. You can keep some of the old ones, but get some new ones of your own. Remember the past, but now you have a new life. We always did Christmas together. That first Christmas Eve after he died, a friend said, 'You'll come to our kids' house and start a new tradition with us.' I did, and it was a joyful Christmas Eve. On his birthday, my family invited me to their home. It was still a celebration. The hardest was Valentine's Day with all the cards displayed and the constant advertising about sweethearts. Our neighbors' church was having a celebration for singles and couples. They invited me, and I went with them and had a great time. The first wedding anniversary after he died was difficult. Then I'd remember the past and have good memories. But this year would have been our fiftieth anniversary, and that was hard. People sent emails to me saying they knew it was hard for me, which helped." Barb W.

"You need to find a balance in deciding between doing things the same way you did in the past or 'shaking it up' with new ways of celebrating. I got my puppy on our first anniversary after his death so I'd have a happy association with that day. A friend advised me that if I was invited to an event on a first, to take my own car so I could allow myself an out if I needed it, if it got to be too stressful." Joyce B.

"The anticipation of a first without him is worse than the actual day. When the day comes around, keep busy. I had to learn to share the holidays with the families of my daughters-in-law." Kathy H.

"That first year was the hardest. We had shared everything. You don't want to be alone. If you have your kids or other people around you, that's good. The kids helped. They were there for all the firsts—the first birthday, our anniversary. They had planned a big fiftieth anniversary party for us, and my husband died three months before our anniversary. We all said he would have wanted the party to go on, so we had the party and put his picture out. I'm glad we did that, had the party." Nancy J.

"Having your dearest friends and family with you will help, although no one will take the place of your husband at that time. I got through the firsts by doing day-to-day stuff. I needed my comfort zone. Christmas is very special to me. It's all about the birth of Jesus, not about us. I took friends to church, and, yes, I missed him, but he's in a better place." Carol L.

"On Thanksgiving I was alone, and I cried. For Christmas I took my dog and traveled to my daughter's home. My widowed friend and I have the same birthday, and we're going to spend it together." Judie N.

"My husband died on our son's birthday. On Christmas I had dinner with the family. I think the second Christmas was harder than the first. My advice is to be with people." Sandy G.

"My advice is to keep busy. Make plans ahead of time, and don't leave anything to chance. Let friends know it's the first. Don't expect family members to call because it's such a disappointment when they don't. My husband died on New Year's Day, and you'd think they'd remember but no calls." Evelyn C.

The Year of "Firsts"

"That year of firsts was really hard. The first Christmas I went to my son's, and we went to church together. I had always gone with my husband. I couldn't wait for that Christmas to be over. On his first birthday following his death, my sons called to see how I was doing. The grieving is not as bad now. My advice is to get out and be with people." Mary B.

"It was very hard in the beginning, but it gets easier. My daughter and I go to the cemetery on his birthday and on our anniversary." Lyn L.

"On those days remember the positives. My friend and I have the same birthday, and together we'll celebrate our first birthday without our husbands." Joan A.

"Be with friends or relatives on those days. I stayed home on Christmas, and it was terrible. Then I spent Christmas with my cousins, and friends also invited me over. New Year's Eve was hard. I hated being alone but felt better when I went out with two of my cousins. If you're alone on your birthday and don't hear from anyone, it makes you sad." Lee M.

"I have no problem with all the firsts. I'm happy my husband is in Heaven." Shirley W.

"My second husband died ten days before Christmas, and I was not in the mood to celebrate. Three of my boys came down for Christmas. I had put up some small lights, and they got a small tree. It's better to be with people or to go out with people. Go to the phone and call someone. The phone is your lifeline." Jan H.

"The toughest day was New Year's Eve because we were 'party people.' Our group of friends would rotate going to one house for dinner, then to another to watch the ball drop in Times Square on TV, then to another house to have dessert. My husband and I were the oldest couple, but we didn't 'poop out' early like the younger couples did. Inviting friends over for other firsts might help." Audrey C.

"Those firsts are hard. I did something new on those days like eating in a new restaurant, something my husband wouldn't have done. I also released five balloons and made a wish with each one I released." Jolene M.

"It didn't get easier. This year was the first time in nine years that my daughter and I had a big Christmas tree. My hobby was collecting ornaments, so I had to do it. We worked it out. We do holidays differently now and don't make traditional meals. I shop for the food, and my daughter cooks. For Thanksgiving, we made lamb chops. On his birthday we go out to eat and then buy a cake. This year I might make his favorite pie, lemon meringue." Lou H.

And a final thought:

"Holidays were hard. I went to the cemetery, said prayers, and talked to him. On these holidays and events, you need to let yourself feel the connection with him and the love. You don't want to give it up, but you have to go on. My husband was in the hospital for my birthday and our anniversary, so I went out to dinner with friends. Then he was in the hospital for Christmas and came home for New Year's Eve. Everything seemed back to normal until he passed in March. I always said the Lord was preparing me for being alone during those times. The first Christmas I put up a Christmas tree because I love Christmas and knew if I didn't do it then, I never would. I also had family over. I started having a cocktail party with friends who were single and in couples. On the anniversary of his death, I'd eat out with friends. I also attend church throughout the Easter week, which is comforting." Barb B.

Ask yourself—

What are my immediate thoughts after reading this chapter "The Year of Firsts"?

_____

_____

_____

_____

_____

Did I find any ideas that might help me get through those first milestones and holidays?

_____

_____

_____

_____

_____

What impressed me most in reading what the women had to say in this chapter?

_____

_____

_____

_____

_____

What advice could I give another woman to help her get through that first year of special occasions and holidays without her husband?

_____

_____

_____

_____

_____

What I want to remember from this chapter:

_____

_____

_____

_____

_____

CHAPTER 12
Paying the Bills & Dealing with Finances

"There Has to Be an Easier Way to Do This!"

Pete and I always had our own checkbooks with both of our names on the checks. He would pay his bills and the major household expenses, and I would pay my bills and give Pete extra money from my salary, and later my teacher's pension, to add to his checking account.

When Pete developed pneumonia and entered the hospital in early March, I took over paying the bills he had paid from his checking account, and that was a rude awakening! I could tell from the White-Out he had used in his check register that he must have been pushing himself to get everything entered as best he could; in hindsight, I believe he could tell he was losing ground with regard to his MDS. Even before that, let's just say that his checkbook system was not my system.

The first thing I needed to do was to change his system to mine. I began by going online and printing out bank

131

statements beginning in December, when his checkbook began losing its neatness and accuracy. I picked up a new check register and, using the printed statements, transferred entries from December through March into it while double-checking Pete's figures. I remember the day my in-laws entered Pete's hospital room and were amused to find me intensely at work over a hospital tray covered with the old and new check registers, a calculator, and several months of checking account statements. Once I had transferred Pete's system to mine, I breathed a sigh of relief.

I still keep "Pete's" checking account and use that for paying household expenses online or by check; I use my checking account to pay my airline charge card on which I charge most everything else: food, gas, pharmacy items, vet bills, car repairs, clothing purchases, etc. We never had any balances on our charge cards because we never charged anything we couldn't pay off at the end of the month, and I continue to follow that guideline. I record everything I charge in a check register kept in my wallet so there are no surprises when I get my charge account statement. When the statement arrives, I check off the charges I've written in the register and balance it as I would with a checking account. It's also a good way to make sure my charge account contains no questionable charges.

The system for paying bills that works best for me is to pay them as they come in. When I get an email alerting me to a bill coming due, I enter my online payment in the checkbook with the due date for that bill and the payment confirmation number. When the printed copy arrives in the mail, I can look in my checkbook and confirm that it's already been paid.

On the advice of my banker, I've transferred my regular savings account to a Money Market account, which will pay me more interest. It's important to have a banker who knows you personally and is able to give good advice and answers to your banking questions. I feel as if my banker Sandy and I have become friends through our interactions since Pete passed.

When I met with our financial advisor to discuss our investments and make necessary changes to our accounts, I took our close friend Dave, a retired CPA, with me. Dave asked pertinent questions, helping me to better understand the investment process. Joe, my Fidelity financial advisor, was not our advisor when Pete was alive. However, I immediately had confidence in Joe's plans for our account and was pleased that he listened to me and respected my opinions.

Because Pete was hospitalized in Florida during March and April, Dave arranged a six-month extension on my income taxes and later prepared them for me. With Pete's passing, my tax situation this year is more complex, and Dave suggested I find another tax preparer. I asked friends and family members for recommendations and from these selected a professional I felt comfortable with. I've received an extension and will meet with my tax preparer when I return to Wisconsin. I'm to bring last year's tax return, all my tax documents that I've received in the mail, my receipts for deductions, and Pete's death certificate to our meeting. These are important papers and are kept where I can quickly find them. In the meantime, I've been paying estimated taxes for the current year. Ask your tax preparer to help you with yours.

I can't stress enough the importance of organization. I have file cabinets in Pete's office and place pocket folders between the file folders. That way I don't have to go through papers in the file drawer because I can remove the entire pocket folder. On the front of the folders, I've used a Magic Marker to write, for example, "Cars" (anything related to my car such as bill of sale, registration, license and plate renewals), "Insurance" (my house, car, and health insurance-related papers), "Fidelity" (any investment-related information), "Taxes" (last year's completed state and federal income tax forms and end-of-the-year summaries for the current year), "Bank" (changes in any accounts, bank statements), "Cancellations" (Pete's cancelled health and accidental death life insurance policies, charge cards, anything I've cancelled since Pete passed), "Social Security" (any papers and correspondence pertaining to the substitution of Pete's Social Security for mine since his was the higher amount), "Funeral" (funeral expenses, death certificates, the obituary and published death notice, plans for the funerals). I have other pocket folders, but these will give you an idea of how you can use them. I keep any loose receipts or papers I'll need for tax deductions in a gallon Ziploc baggie marked "Tax Deductions" and the year; that's kept in the file cabinet with the pocket folders.

Remember to update any wills or trusts. If you don't have your own attorney, ask people you trust for recommendations. This is definitely something you need to discuss with a reputable attorney who is familiar with trusts.

If you're unsure as to where your husband had his financial dealings, you may have to wait for statements to arrive in the mail, so carefully read any mail that arrives in his name from financial institutions. It's also a good idea to check any safety deposit box you may have. Do not destroy any mail or papers that may contain important information.

The following tips and advice from women who have been widowed are helpful in setting up a system to pay bills and dealing with financial investments. Their intent is to help you manage the money you're going to be living on.

"I paid some of the bills before my husband died. Now I pay online or through auto-pay. Be sure you have your husband's passwords to access his accounts. A lot of bills aren't mailed to you because they come through online. When I was alone, I had to develop a system because I would forget to pay them. It's easy to procrastinate when you're alone. You have to be organized because now you're the one accountable. Make a system and stick to it. Here's mine—I keep a journal book divided by months. I write checks on the first and the fifteenth of the month. In my journal I write what's due, when it's due, if I paid by check or auto-pay, and when I paid it. Then I can see if I paid the bill and if any bill increased from last year. I can see what's due on the first and what's due on the fifteenth." Kathy H.

"Look after yourself first, second, and third! Make sure you understand your finances. Go to your banker and talk often. Double-check everything. Be sure you've cancelled all your husband's credit cards and checking accounts. Someone was hacking into my husband's account twenty-four hours after he passed. Have a good financial advisor. Hopefully, have someone in the family or a friend you can talk to about financial matters. Check with the insurance company, and ask for help when you need it. Get everything in your name. It was easier for me because I paid the bills before my husband passed. I pay ninety percent of the bills through my checking account. Some of the bills are on auto-pay, like the electric, charge cards, and cable. For the rest of the bills, I look at the due dates and pay them. At times, I'll post-date the check. I try to stay offline in paying bills. The rent for my house and my insurance are paid right away even though they're not due yet, and I post-date the checks." Angie O.

"Be organized! Do a budget; month to month might be easier for you. List what you have to pay out and what is coming in. You need an idea of what you're going to spend. I pay my bills before the due date. I don't use the computer, so I write checks for everything. I had paid all the bills and did our taxes before my husband died. He handled all our financial accounts and took care of the cars. After he passed, if I needed guidance with finances or cars, I asked our friend's son for advice. He works in finance and also knows cars. If you've never written a check or balanced a checkbook, you can get help from family members, friends, or your banker. If you decide to do your own taxes, the IRS has people to help you. Banks have retired CPAs who come in to help, and senior citizen centers also have help around tax time. Otherwise, you can go to a tax preparer." Barb B.

"I had handled all our bills before, so it wasn't difficult for me when he passed. Know the due dates for your bills. I would pay them a week before their due dates." Debbi C.

"I open the bills when they come in. If they're paid with auto-pay, I'll write that on the envelope. If they're not paid with auto-pay, I'll write the due date on the envelope." Kay P.

"My husband liked to pay the bills. Three years before he died, I noticed he was missing little things with finances, so I did a spreadsheet. He said he wanted me to go to our financial planner alone so I'd understand our financial situation more and get to know the person. You have to be aware of your finances. You can't be a spendthrift because your money has to last. It's always good to do a budget so you know where you stand. Think ahead. When I sold the house and bought a condo five years after he passed, I could have gotten an expensive condo. Instead I bought a condo for half of what I sold the house for so I'd have money left over to work for me. I had never done our taxes before. Now I take all the tax information to my tax man. In the past I made mistakes but lived to tell about them. One year, for some reason, I didn't receive my 1099 tax form. The next year I had to pay money because of that. Another time I made an insurance payment for less than I should have. The first notification I had of doing that was when the insurance company sent me a threatening letter saying if I didn't pay, they'd cut off my insurance, so be sure the amount you write on your checks is the correct amount. I auto-pay a lot. You have to realize there can be changes with insurance payments or pensions. You have to be prepared. When I received a letter telling me my husband's insurance from the state was going to be cancelled, I interviewed three insurance companies. If you don't want to do it alone, have someone sit with you. Don't be afraid to ask for help." Lila S.

"Organize yourself. Check the due dates and pay the bills when they come in. I took care of all the bills before my husband died. A friend of mine never did anything like that and now has to ask her children to help her." Ginny G.

"I pay the bills on the phone as soon as they come in. I like paying online. I don't do auto-pay. My husband was a financial advisor. After he died, I interviewed six different companies before deciding upon one. Be very careful not to invest with any individuals. You need to be able to get statements from a reputable, established financial company, not an individual like Bernie Madoff, who stole money from investors, including widows. Get recommendations for a good financial advisor from a reputable financial company. Get a living trust." Beverly K.

"I suggest you make a list of bills and their due dates. You'll be able to see if they've been paid and will know if, for whatever reason, you haven't received the bill in the mail. If you have your list of due dates, you can call the company and tell them the due date is getting close, and you haven't received your bill. One night I suddenly realized I didn't have fire insurance. The next day I called the insurance company and didn't go with the company my husband had had." Pearl G.

"I'd been paying the bills before my husband passed. I check the due date but don't pay as soon as the bills come in. I'll wait until I have a few and then pay them because some bills trickle in later. I write checks for all the bills except for the phone, which I pay with auto-pay because I get a larger percentage of reward points through the bank for the phone. When I write checks, I don't have anything coming out of my debit and don't have to check on the computer. For me, paying bills by check gives me more control. I want to know at all times what I have in my checking account and when I have it. I may not be able to get on my computer for some reason to pay bills, but I always have access to my checking account. I think the only advantage to paying bills online is you can pay if you're away when the bill comes due. Sometimes you're away, and then you can get caught with an overdue charge. If I know I'm going to be traveling, I'll double up on my payment and then I'll get a credit on my account. Be organized doing whatever works for you. If you haven't been paying the bills, you'll ask someone for help and will probably pay as they suggest, by checks, online, or auto-pay, because they've taken you under their wing. If you've never written a check, you can ask a family member or friend for help, or if you don't want to ask them, you can ask someone at the bank who hears this all the time." Joanne W.

"When you pay your bills depends upon how many checks you have coming in each month and when they come in. I pay my bills as soon as I get them. Don't put them away before you pay them because it's too easy to forget about them. I personally don't care for auto-pay because I like to write the checks so I can see what I have." Nancy J.

"Find people you trust—a banker, financial advisor, attorney. Don't be afraid to check your credit score. I paid all the household bills, and my husband handled our investments. I was in the habit of paying the bills once a month because that's how he was paid. Do whatever works for you in setting up a budget. I have to wait six more years to collect his social security. I was shocked at how long the process was to close the estate. If your mortgage rate is lower than what you can earn at the bank, don't pay it off. Leave the money in the bank. Look at all your options. Don't give up all things in your life. Some things have to be taken care of right away and others don't." Joyce B.

"I'm getting more bills auto-deducted, but I'm not real comfortable with people subtracting money from my bank account. I gave our cottage to our church, who had been renting it from us, and now I just pay the taxes. Ask a trusted family member for advice. Be sure you have a good lawyer, but legal services can be expensive." Kay J.

"Know your finances—what's coming in and what's going out. I had a lot of challenges at first after my husband passed. The Florida utility company kept taking money out of our auto-pay, and I didn't even live in that state anymore. I had to drive three hours to the bank to get them to stop the automatic withdrawal. Be organized! If you need help, talk to friends and ask, 'How do I do this?' If you've never written a check before, ask someone at the bank or friends how to do it. If you want to learn more about finances, you can take courses at a tech school. A women's center will sometimes help women transition from being a housewife to someone who is now the one taking care of finances. Always be wary of scams, especially younger or older men who want to help you. Do not accept offers that are unsolicited by mail or over the phone. Get your own Realtor, not someone who calls you. Remember, if it sounds too good to be true, it usually is." Bobbi V.

"I pay most of my bills through auto-pay. Your bank will explain it to you and set it up for you so you won't have to worry about a bill statement getting misplaced when it comes in. I always did all the banking and bookwork." Shirley W.

"I went online to set up auto-pay for many of the bills. You need to make sure cash is in your account. I was the bookkeeper for our business. When I sold the business, I was the one who had to complete the deal. It's important to have a good lawyer (mine knew my husband) because your mind isn't your normal mind. It's easy to get distracted in the beginning of your loss. It's important to have a trust so you don't have to go through probate. I used my husband's life insurance to put money down on a house for my daughter and me that had the smallest yard and driveway to take care of. My daughter owns the house and pays some of the bills. I pay the cell phone and my charge card." Lou H.

"I pay all my bills online." Judie N.

"Develop a good support system with your bank and financial advisor. Ask if they have experience in dealing with widows. You need to be diligent, get guidance, and have good people in your corner. Document everything! I have two lists—one for when my bills are due and the second that has all my passwords to everything. I get my bills online. Be organized! Don't be afraid to ask questions and ask for help from your banker and financial advisor. You are responsible for your financial future. You need a plan so your money doesn't run out. Watch your dollars!" Evelyn C.

"Make paying your bills as convenient as possible. I pay them when they come in because no one knows what tomorrow will bring. I have as much as I can paid automatically by auto-pay out of my checking account. Your bank can arrange that." Carol L.

"I used to work in a bank and always paid the bills, so there's no change there. My advice is to talk to professionals. If you don't know how to do something, ask at the bank, 'How do I write a check?' If you're computer savvy, Google how to do something. I write checks for the bills as they come in and don't pay over the Internet. I was so young when I was widowed, fifty-nine, and I couldn't get any funds until I was fifty-nine and a half. When my husband died, I didn't even know he had a life insurance policy. I had to borrow the money for his funeral from my mother-in-law, whom I paid back. Things work out, but you have to be patient. You learn to step up and do what you have to do; adrenaline takes over. I've made arrangements for all my money to go to my daughter because of what a friend's daughter went through when her mom died." Lyn L.

"When we were first married, my husband gave me the checkbook and said, 'Here. It's your job now.' I also did our taxes. Find someone you trust to help you make financial decisions." Joan A.

"I always paid the bills and did all the bookwork for our business. It's fortunate that I'm computer savvy. I never thought I'd ever get involved with technology, but I took several computer classes which are offered at senior centers. For the past two or three years, I've had my groceries delivered. I go online to order, and the store brings the groceries to my home. I had trouble with the insurance company, and my sons helped and guided me through getting it resolved. So many times I've said to my husband, 'Help me!' I pay the bills when they come in because when you're alone, it's too easy to get sidetracked. The interest is very high if you don't pay your bills on time." Mary B.

"The minute I get the bills, I write the due date on the front of the envelope and pay it as soon as possible. I keep one folder for the bills from one state I live in and one folder for the bills from the other state." Gladi B.

"I keep my bills in one place and pay them as soon as they come in." Carole C.

"Find someone to teach you if you don't know how to manage finances or pay bills. It wasn't hard for me because I had done it before." Marijo Z.

"I pay most of my bills online because I travel a lot. Some of the expenses I'll pay all at once, like my car or insurance, so I don't have to think about the payments. Every month my house payment is taken out of my account through auto-pay. I pay other bills online five days before they're due so the companies aren't using my money. I need to get a new financial advisor. I'm not comfortable with the one I have now. He's younger and talks down to me, 'the widow.' I feel as if he doesn't treat me with respect. He wants to manage all my money and give me an allowance each month. I want a different advisor. Right now, I'm doing my financial accounts myself and don't feel real confident about it." Lee M.

"My husband and I had a joint account, and then I had to pay all the bills. I had his name removed from the checks nine months after he passed. Everything in its time. I pay my bills a couple of days before the due date. I keep a personal monthly calendar and write the due dates for bills and their amounts. Then I check the bills off after I pay them. Now I'm paying more online." Jolene M.

"I had to step in and take over paying the bills when his illness took over. I paid them online. Be aware of due dates!" Ruby C.

"Give thought to your financial decisions. Be organized. I pay bills online. Set up a budget and get to know your budget. You can also set up an automatic bill pay at the bank. Asking for help is the hardest thing for me to do, but I do it." Sandy G.

"I'm fortunate. My daughter and her husband take care of my bills. Right now, she's fighting with the company that sends me my husband's pension because they want to cut it." Audrey C.

"If you haven't paid bills before, line them up so you know what needs to be paid first. I keep a list of regular due dates for certain bills in the back of my checkbook, not on a computer. I wait until a week before they're due to pay them. Some are on auto-pay through the bank. For the others, I'll call the company and pay them over the phone." Jan B.

And a final thought:

"If you're younger, say, under seventy, you'll figure it out. If you're older, you might have no clue as to paying bills or finances. If you don't know how things get paid, ask for help. If you've never written a check or balanced a checkbook, your bank will help you. I worked in a bank, and saw there are many women who have never done this. You should ask a professional, a CPA or banker, if you don't want to share your lack of knowledge with family members or friends. There are also bookkeeping services. You can Google them or ask a CPA for a referral. These services will take your bills and make out the checks for you to sign. They do not sign your checks. They will also balance your checkbook or set up automatic withdrawals." Barb W.

Ask yourself—

After reading this chapter "Paying the Bills and Dealing with Finances," what are my immediate thoughts?

_____

_____

_____

_____

_____

I think the most helpful tips I read for paying bills are:

_____

_____

_____

_____

Some things I hadn't thought of with regard to paying bills and handling finances are:

_____

_____

_____

_____

_____

Advice I could give to a woman who is now paying her bills and responsible for her own finances would be:

_____

_____

_____

_____

_____

What I want to remember from this chapter:

_____

_____

_____

_____

_____

First Photo taken of us together shortly after we began dating – 1972.

Our Informal Wedding – April 13, 1974.

"60's Prom" Themed Party – 1980's.

Acapulco Vacation – 1990's.

*Our 2008 Christmas
card photo.*

*At the Renewal of our Wedding Vows on our
35th wedding anniversary – April, 2009.*

*"Roaring 20's"
Themed
Party – 2012.*

Our 2012 Christmas card photo.

Watching July 4th fireworks - 2013

At a hot air balloon festival – 2015.

Our 2015 Christmas card photo.

Christmas with Riley & Murphy – 2016.

Our 2017 Christmas card- We needed to leave this party in Ft. Myers, Florida early because Pete was feeling the effects of chemo. He had insisted on attending.

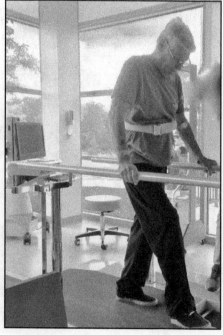

Pete's body reacted to the last chemo he was able to have. He worked so hard in rehab. — Wisconsin, July, 2017.

Pete on his electric scooter – We didn't know this would be his last month at home – Ft. Myers, Florida – February, 2018.

Celebrating our 44th wedding anniversary on April 13th at table #13 in the rehab dining room – Ft. Myers, Florida, 2018.

*In the rehab
courtyard –
2 1/2 weeks
before Pete
was to have
returned home
– April, 2018.*

*Last photo of us taken together 2 weeks before
Pete passed. Rehab courtyard, April, 2018.*

Riley & Murphy on the day Pete passed. I was given the quilt that had covered Pete in hospice. May 15, 2018.

My 2018 Christmas card photo with Riley & Murphy. Ft. Myers, Florida.

CHAPTER 13
Making Decisions

"Are You Going to Sell the House?"
"What About That Leaking Roof?"

Once you become a widow, the questions will begin—"Are you going to sell the house?" (or condo, or move from the apartment) being one of the inquiries you'll hear most often. Those people who mean well are simply asking because they're curious as to what changes, if any, you'll be making now that you're without your husband. No matter the motive behind the question, "I haven't decided yet what I'm going to do" is always a good response and should end any discussion you don't care to continue. If the person asking persists, you can end the interrogation with "Let's talk about something else." I've heard of people asking new widows about selling their homes to get leads for friends or family members in the real estate business. Personally, I think that's crossing a line. Never answer any question you feel is intrusive, and don't allow yourself to be pressured into doing something that doesn't feel right. I know we've been brought up to be polite, but if the person persisting isn't being courteous, you have the right to end the confrontation by excusing yourself and walking away.

Always listen to that little internal voice telling you, "Don't rush in to anything." Shortly after Pete passed, the mail I received included numerous postcards and letters beginning with "Hi, Merryfield Family, I WANT TO BUY YOUR HOUSE AT..." and then my address would be printed underneath. To paraphrase the message, they would give me a guaranteed "fair" offer in forty-eight hours, close on my home ("as is") whenever I was ready, and promised I'd have "no fees and no commissions to worry about." All of this would be "hassle-free" for me. Reading these made me feel as if I were already being hassled by someone attempting to pounce on me and my home. I even suspected the person or company sending out those requests made a practice of getting leads from obituaries, which would be beyond despicable should it be true. Always consult a friend, family member, or the Better Business Bureau if any inquiry is causing you concern. The scam/fraud division of your local police department will give you advice if you're uncertain about any solicitation and may even investigate if your complaint or concern warrants it.

You may have heard that you should wait a year before making any major decisions, such as selling your home or moving, and, basically, that's good advice. However, sometimes other decisions need to be made before that year is up.

When I returned to Wisconsin that spring after Pete passed, I found a water stain next to the skylight we had replaced before leaving for Florida the previous fall. It must have taken months for water to seep through the drywall on the ceiling. There was another water stain in the corner of the dining room ceiling, which meant I had to find someone to locate the source of the leaks and repair it. I called a few roofing companies for quotes that ranged from high to higher.

Wanting additional estimates, I went online, checked our neighborhood website, and found Mike, a multitalented handyman who had excellent reviews of his work. I called him, and for a reasonable price, Mike did a great job repairing the drywall damage and repainting the walls. He also arranged for a reputable roofer to replace five rows of shingles and install new flashing and snow/ice barriers, all at a very fair price. No more leaks. Other repairs that couldn't wait a year needed to be made around the house, repairs that Pete had been unable to do once his health began to decline. Mike handled these repairs and did such an outstanding job that my friends and neighbors began hiring him for work at their homes. They all agreed that I had done well in finding such a great handyman.

There are major and minor decisions that you'll need to make, and reading how women who have been widowed have handled their decision-making may help you in yours.

"Don't make any major decisions right away. Give yourself time to grieve, to accept the newness of your life. You don't want to make a mistake and then regret it. The biggest decision you want to make is to not get remarried right away. You don't want to go from a widow to a divorcée. When you need to make a decision, bounce it off friends. Have a good financial person and a good tax preparer. Never tell anyone your personal finances. You can generalize but don't go into detail." Kathy H.

"As time goes by, you may find, as I did, that you've grown into a different person, and it may be time to make some changes. I talked to a man about a water heater, and he wanted to tell me what to do. I didn't want him to dictate to me. I wanted him to give me options so I could process them. Every man wanted to tell me what I should do, so I stopped talking to them. When I told my aunt that I didn't approve of the job the snow removal service was doing, she said, 'Let it go.' Know when to do that. You're probably used to making decisions with your husband and discussing what you want to do. Now it's only you." Pearl G.

"A cousin of my husband's asked if I was selling the house. I said, 'I'm not going anywhere.' He also tried to get me to sell my husband's car. Don't make any big decisions for one year. Give yourself time to get through that year of fog. Give yourself time to figure things out. You won't know right away, for example, if you want to sell his car. You'll be amazed at what you can do." Joyce B.

"Do not make any major decisions for the first year. People asked if I was going to sell the house, and I really thought I'd sell it within the first five years. Then sixteen years later I'm still here because the thought of going through thirty years of stuff in the crawlspace is too daunting. I pay to have the lawn and driveway done. I make my own decisions about remodeling. You can always ask a relative or friend for references; my remodeling guy gave me the name of a plumber. I asked someone at Ace Hardware for a plumber referral, and he said he was a licensed plumber and gave me his card. I asked my brother-in-law for advice on where to go to have my garage door fixed. My son knows a lot of tradespeople. You should ask someone you know for a referral before you go to the Yellow Pages. Does that still even exist?" Joanne W.

"Do not succumb to pressure. Be very cautious. Take your time and look at all aspects and all variables. Don't just think about what you want, but ask yourself what will happen if you do something. Not making a decision is in itself a decision. I'm a quick decision-maker, but when I'm grieving, I tell myself to STOP!" Bobbi V.

"I don't think you should make major decisions for the first year. Let everything repeat itself once. You can make a wish list, but don't do anything on it for a year. I made the decision myself to build a new house two years after my husband died. No one in my family even knew I had bought the lot." Debbi C.

"Wait before making major decisions like selling property. If you're not comfortable about doing something, talk to an attorney or someone else you trust. I didn't listen to people who tried to tell me what to do. I gave my car to my niece. I kept our vacation home for a year, then transferred it to my name. I stayed in our condo and did some remodeling." Barb B.

"Don't be rushed or pressured. Don't let people tell you what to do. A professional or friend can help. Sell the house or car when you're ready. I made my decisions myself." Barb W.

"When I sold my home in Wisconsin and decided to move to The Villages in Florida, after the kids took what they needed, I sold all my furniture. I went to estate sales, bargain and treasures stores, and thrift stores to buy the furniture for my Florida home. I didn't need to buy new. I make my own decisions but ask my sons for advice. They're younger and smarter than I am, and that makes a difference because the decisions I make will affect them in one way or another." Angie O.

"I make my own decisions. I sold our Florida condo to get capital to earn money for me. When I eventually decide to sell the house, I'll get an apartment." Kay P.

"I make all my own decisions and rarely involve the kids. I bought my car myself. My kids thanked me for being so independent and taking the pressure off them. However, if I need them, they're there." Lila S.

"Wait! Be careful. Don't rush in to anything. You have time. You can make mistakes because every widow will make mistakes. I made the decision to move from Michigan to Florida full time, and I'm glad I did that. I had asked the Lord for confirmation of my decision." Beverly K.

"I make my own decisions. My son wanted to go with me to buy a different car, and I said I'd do it myself." Shirley W.

"I called someone to cut down a tree and didn't call the kids for help. People would ask me if I was going to sell the house and move to a condo. I said no. I felt warmth when I was in our home. My relatives let me do my own thing and say I am a strong lady. If you don't know something, ask for ideas. You can hire a handyman, but you can fix a lot of things yourself. If, for example, your toilet breaks, you can go online to YouTube and look up 'how to fix a toilet.' Home Depot is a good resource for plumbers, etc. I have a neighbor who says to call him first before I call a professional. I learned how to put the windshield washer fluid in the car, something my husband would always do. My daughter said my husband would have been proud of me, that he would have spent more time on the golf course if he had known I could do everything I've done!" Ginny G.

"I decided not to sell the house because I have wonderful memories there. My eyesight isn't good, and if I lose it, I can walk the house myself. If I have a major decision to make, I'll talk to my kids and discuss it with them." Nancy J.

"I make my decisions on my own. I gave our cottage to the church that had been renting it. I told the kids why I was thinking of doing this, and they agreed with my decision. It didn't cause a money squabble with the kids. My daughter sees my bank statement and knows what's going on. Some women start spending money, but I'm frugal and have never been a big spender." Kay J.

"If you really need help, go to someone qualified. I make my decisions by myself but might ask my kids for suggestions." Carol L.

"Wait a year before making any major decisions because your mind isn't normal and plays tricks on you. I made some poor decisions, but they weren't the worst. For example, I sold a rowboat for less than I should have. I had a big rummage sale, and some people tried to steal items. My brother-in-law helped me set up for the rummage, and an old friend organized the sales and dealt with the people. My daughter helps pick out and buys the appliances for our home; she's a life saver. I'll talk things over with her like what to do with family items from her grandparents. My health insurance was terrible and cost over $1300.00 a month. My mind was frozen, and I couldn't make myself switch companies. My lawyer helped me get the cost down." Lou H.

"I needed a new air conditioner and bought it myself." Judie N.

"The hardest thing is to move to make the decisions. You have to motivate yourself to make a decision like deciding to buy a new dishwasher. My husband and I hadn't dealt with downsizing when he was alive. We always made our decisions together, and now I'm the one making the decisions." Sandy G.

"Before my husband died, we had looked for a house for eight years. Within that first year, I bought a house for my son and me." Carole C.

"Many people asked if I was going to sell the house and move to a condo. I'd ask, 'Why would I do that?' I have a smaller house and pay for things to be repaired as I go. Why would I move to a condo and pay HOA (homeowners' association) fees?" Lyn L.

"I needed a new air conditioner and bought it. My daughters are wonderful but sometimes try to be parents." Karen C.

"Don't make major decisions that first year. Don't tell others what you're thinking of doing because some will try to change your mind." Ruby C.

"Do what you think is right. You can still listen to people, especially those with recent experience, for instance, when you're buying a car. After my husband died, my daughter thought I would sell the house and started packing up everything. I said I didn't want to sell the house in New York. I have good friends there, and my church is there. The house is a two-story and is getting to be a lot to take care of. It's expensive to keep up. I'll take it one year at a time. I've thought of going into a condo because it would be easier for me, but I don't have to move. I'll take this summer and see how it goes for five months." Audrey C.

"I haven't had to make any big decisions so far." Jan B.

"I'm very independent but bad at making decisions. I'm a Libra, so I go back and forth in my decision-making. Another Libra will understand. I'm impulsive and second-guess myself. I like others' opinions but make my own decisions. A year after my husband died, a friend called and said I didn't sound good and told me to come to Ohio for the summer. I bought a trailer to live in and sold it after four or five years. I want to do something different." Lee M.

"My husband loved cars and was waiting for a car to come in. I bought the car he had wanted to buy, and I'm happy with it. I needed a new air conditioner and bought it." Joan A.

"My husband was in the hospital so much that there was a lot we had prepared for, but we had never prepared for death. I was alone so much and had to make the decision to buy a different car because I was afraid the car would break down driving back and forth to the hospital. I sold the house and bought a condo. After two years, I felt better. I was given the strength to make the decisions I needed to make." Mary B.

"You now have to make the decisions. When you need to make a decision, give it time and ponder it. Sit on it. Sleep on it. Be proactive rather than reactive. Get back to it after you've done some thinking." Evelyn C.

"Give yourself time. Consider all the angles. Your new normal is different than the old. My husband had insisted on paying off our house before he died, and I'm very grateful for that. My major decision was not to make any major decisions. Things have to evolve; let them play out and fall into place. When people would ask me if I was going to sell the house, that didn't bother me. I'd rather they say something silly or insensitive than nothing at all. I made the decision to bring my husband's car to Florida." Jolene M.

And a final thought:

"Wait at least a year before making any major decisions. You have to give it time. You'll have a better idea of what to do later. With regard to minor decisions, if you can't make it yourself, ask other people's opinions. You'll make some right decisions and some wrong, and you'll have to deal with those. I made the decision to start my own bed-and-breakfast. Everything had to be perfect. I needed to be taking care of people, and I was the hostess. I gained self-confidence and self-esteem." Marijo Z.

Ask yourself—

What are my immediate thoughts after reading this chapter on "Making Decisions"?

_____

_____

_____

_____

Am I confident with regard to making decisions myself?

_____

_____

_____

_____

If I'm not confident in my decision-making, who are those I would ask for input?

_____

_____

_____

_____

_____

What are some decisions I might need to make now or in the future?

_____

_____

_____

_____

_____

How am I going to go about making those decisions?

_____

_____

_____

_____

_____

What advice would I give someone newly widowed on making decisions?

_____

_____

_____

_____

What I want to remember from this chapter:

_____

_____

_____

CHAPTER 14
Cooking & Eating for One

(In a Pinch, There's Always Peanut Butter & Jelly)

If there's someone living at home with you, you've continued to cook for more than one person even though your husband is no longer there. You may not be making his favorite dishes if other members of the family didn't care for them, but you still have others to consider when you're shopping and planning meals. If, however, you had been cooking meals for just you and your husband, you may need to put more thought into planning meals now that you're usually the only one eating.

When Pete was alive, I'd have V-8 juice and multigrain cereal with half a banana for breakfast, and that remains my morning meal. For lunch I'll whip up a large protein shake in the blender using almond milk, yogurt, whey protein powder, a shake of flax seed, greens, half a banana, and frozen peach slices. If I have fresh fruit, I'll throw that into the mix. Then it's time for the evening meal, and that's not as easy as the other two.

Any of our friends reading this are probably laughing because Pete used to say, "Bonnie's favorite thing to make for dinner is reservations." While we did enjoy eating out when he was feeling better, we ate at home more often as Pete's energy began to wane. I'm not even close to being a gourmet cook, so it's fortunate that Pete liked meals that were traditionally simple, such as salads, burgers, steak with a baked potato, grilled cheese and tomato soup, meat loaf, BBQ sandwiches, chili, and his favorite, pizza. He could have eaten pizza every day and been perfectly happy.

Now that I'm living alone, I make an effort to put more thought into what I'll be eating for dinner. When I eat dinner out, the servings are usually so large that I'll eat half the meal and bring the rest home for the next day. Sometimes I think the inside of my refrigerator looks like it's growing Styrofoam when those take-home containers begin to accumulate.

If I make something like a casserole or spaghetti and meatballs, I'll divide it into small portions which I'll freeze for future meals. When I made a pot roast for company, I had enough left over to freeze in plastic baggies. I always have hardboiled eggs in the refrigerator. You can eat those during the day or use them to make an egg salad sandwich. I'll also make six salmon patties and divide them into two-patty portions to freeze. I've also discovered Bear Creek creamy wild rice soup, and I'll substitute one cup of low-sodium chicken broth for one of the eight cups of water. I'll make a chicken breast, shred it, and add that to the base. It is a really delicious meal. It lasts for two to three days, and there's enough left to freeze for future meals.

While writing this introduction, I'll admit I was eager for meal suggestions from others living alone. Many did admit that a peanut butter and jelly sandwich is their go-to meal when they've put off shopping for groceries, and it certainly is mine.

Women who have been widowed have excellent suggestions when you're cooking and eating for one.

"I'm very conscious of eating nutritionally, and I suggest freezing a chicken breast after dividing it into thirds. You'll have enough for three meals, and you can add vegetables, potatoes, a salad, whatever you want. BLTs (bacon, lettuce, & tomato sandwiches) on whole-grain bread are good. For snacks, I'll have almonds and walnuts or celery sticks that I dip in hummus; I buy the hummus in single-serving packets to avoid opening one large container that might spoil before I can finish it." Gladi B.

"My cooking habits changed little because while my husband was sick, I was already cooking for one. I'd make a lot to try to get him to eat. I froze a lot of meals." Debbi C.

"If I go to lunch, I'll eat something I wouldn't cook at home. I go out to eat often. Sloppy joes are easy to make, and you can divide it into two servings and freeze for later. I'll eat cheese and crackers a lot. The cheese is protein. Try not to have sweets or snacks like chips around the house. They're too easy to grab when you're hungry, and they're not nutritional." Kay J.

"It's a challenge. Try to eat healthy. If you don't like to eat alone, invite a friend over. My husband was away for work a lot, so I was often cooking just for myself. If I'm out, I'll eat a big lunch and then something little for dinner." Beverly K.

"It's hard. I'm a lot looser about what I eat. I'll make a Cornish hen with Brownberry stuffing (add a little butter for moisture), and you can put the leftover stuffing on a pork chop for another meal. I'll make soups, which you can eat for two days and then freeze the rest." Kay P.

"Buy only what you need so you don't waste food. You're not buying for two anymore. If you like to cook, have friends over. When you cook, you can freeze half of what you make. You can take food to someone who needs it; for example, I took food to someone who gets Meals on Wheels during the week but doesn't get them on weekends. If you don't like to cook, you can go to senior meal programs. I like to cook, so I bought a full freezer and freeze a lot of food." Barb B.

"You can still cook the same amount, but freeze portions. I'll share with my children's families, who appreciate it because they're busy, and it saves them having to cook. I find cooking to be therapeutic and distracting. I'll sit down on Saturday or Sunday and write my schedule for the upcoming week on a calendar, or a spiral binder could be used. If I see that I'll be late getting home on one day, I'll take something out of the freezer. If I've forgotten to do that, I'll defrost it in the micro. I could also stop for dinner or have a peanut butter and jelly sandwich." Pearl G.

"We both loved to cook. Now food doesn't mean as much to me. I eat a lot of prepared food. I'll eat lunch out. If I go out to dinner, I'll order steak because I don't make that at home." Joyce B.

"I do cook but eat more frozen food. You have to buy smaller quantities of food. Otherwise, you'll be throwing a lot of food out. I don't eat a lot of fast foods. I'll make chicken Kiev and have it with a baked potato. You can buy a single potato wrapped in plastic to microwave. You can buy one steak or ask the butcher for just one. You can cook a chicken breast, soup, individual mac and cheese servings. I keep hardboiled eggs in the refrigerator. You can make spaghetti or have a sandwich. I'll buy a bag of pasta with vegetables and add frozen vegetables to it." Lila S.

"Make a meal and freeze part of it. My daughter lives with me, so I'm not cooking for just me." Shirley W.

"At the beginning, I didn't do much cooking. I only cooked if I was invited to someone's home for a meal. I ate a lot of popcorn. If I had lunch with friends, I'd have a smaller dinner. Sometimes I'd get Chinese food." Barb W.

"It's hard. I bought a smaller freezer that fits in the laundry room. I make larger portions and freeze half. I cook for myself, so I can eat what I want. It's expensive to eat out. Since my husband passed, I use less seasoning and eat less meat. You can't make a small steak or small roast because it doesn't taste as good. If I go out, I'll order a steak sandwich. I like soups, which are easy on the stomach. Sandra Lee's

Semi-Homemade TV show was good for ideas. I always keep a chicken breast around. You can cut it up, brown it, and add what you want to make a meal. Alessi Sicilian lentil soup is a good base, and to it you can add half a package of frozen peas and carrots, and chopped, browned chicken. You can buy Bear Creek soups online if you can't find them in a store. It's easier to find the creamy wild rice and the minestrone soups. I like creamy wild rice soup and add broth instead of water and then add frozen mixed vegetables." Angie O.

"My eating habits changed after my husband died. I eat smaller portions, like appetizer-size. You develop your own eating habits as time passes. Restaurant food has too much sodium. I still cook and freeze food. I'll have hardboiled eggs, a lot of salads. A big chicken breast can last me three days. I'll still cook big meals for my children and for company." Ginny G.

"The benefit is you can now eat whatever and whenever you want. Cooking for one isn't a problem for me. I eat three meals a day. With Type 2 diabetes, I don't eat the way I did before. Now I have a problem when I have to cook for more people. For breakfast, I might have a bowl of cereal (Cheerios), fruit, Kellogg's and Eggo both have a good breakfast sandwich. For lunch, I'll mix tuna fish or chicken, celery, onion, dill relish, and mayo and put it in the fridge for a sandwich. For dinner, I'll have fish or chicken, fresh or frozen vegetables. I might have a chicken alfredo pizza. I'll buy the cheddar/broccoli soup in the two-quart two-pack at Costco. You get two meals out of one container. I'll make one, and it's very filling. I'll have yogurt or strawberries. I don't eat rice or pasta. The bread I buy is sixteen carbs for two slices." Joanne W.

"I never went to a restaurant for lunch or dinner alone. You can go to Fresh Market and get a small turkey breast or a small chicken breast. That will last two to three days. You can add a chef's salad to that. I can't eat fast food. You can order chicken noodle soup to go. Watch your drinking when you're widowed because you're vulnerable. If you drink, you can talk too much. You have to be careful if someone shows an interest in you." Kathy H.

"Learn to cook smaller portions. Cooking isn't a problem for me because I need a gluten-free diet. I don't eat standing or walking around. I'll put down a place mat and sit at the table and watch TV while I'm eating. You can make a full meal and freeze half of it. I eat fish and chicken once a week. One to two times weekly I'll go to lunch with friends." Carol L.

"Go with the flow. After my husband died, I cooked sometimes and catered to my moods. I had lots of food in the freezer. Keep protein shakes on hand or make them yourself. You can't make good decisions if you're not taking care of yourself. I do a lot of canning and work hard preparing food. It makes it easier for later when I need food for a meal." Bobbi V.

"My husband was a meat-and-potatoes guy. Now I'm experimenting and making meals he wouldn't have liked. I'll divide what I make and freeze portions." Joan A.

"It's the hardest thing. The more you get away from cooking, the more you forget. I don't do a lot of cooking unless the kids are coming over. I'll go to lunch with a girlfriend once weekly where we get a free slice of pie. I'll eat Weight Watchers meals, but those have a high sodium content. I try to cook a meal at least once a week, and I'll make chili or meat loaf and freeze half. It's hard to cook for one." Nancy J.

"At first, I didn't eat much. I'd pick at my food. I'd eat celery and peanut butter. The first thing I ordered when I felt like eating was a pizza." Judie N.

"I live with my daughter, and we eat differently than when my husband was alive. We don't eat potatoes or as much meat, but we eat a lot of vegetables. We'll use cheese instead of butter." Lou H.

"I had to stop eating too much. For breakfast, I'll have an egg, oatmeal, toast, coffee. That becomes lunch if I play pickleball first thing in the morning. For dinner, I'll have stir-fry and sauté fresh zucchini, and pasta. I'll sauté half an avocado with a chopped onion, carrot, fresh vegetables, and scramble it with an egg. I'll eat pre-made fresh stuff and make hamburger patties." Sandy G.

"The first time I was widowed, I had four kids, so I cooked for a lot of people. Now I'll make a steak or lamb chops, a salad, and potato. Sometimes I'll have oatmeal for dinner. I hate frozen foods. Go to the grocery store and buy what you like. I'll eat soup two or three nights a week. Bear Creek soups are good. The deli department has dinners." Marijo Z.

"My oldest son lives with me. I don't do a lot of cooking. We eat salads and prepared meals." Carole C.

"I have no problem and cook for myself a lot. I'll freeze small packets of whatever I make for future meals. I eat a lot of soup. A Crock-Pot is good to use when you live alone. If I go to lunch with girlfriends, I'll bring half of what I ordered home. In eight years I've never gone out to dinner alone." Lee M.

"I'll cook dinner for myself three days a week. Dinner might be frozen chicken patties, a baked potato, and salad. Cauliflower tots are good." Ruby C.

"I think it's horrible to cook for one person. It's very hard. It doesn't pay to make dinner when you're eating alone. Invite people to eat with you. A friend was visiting, and I said she should stay for dinner. I had a pizza in the freezer. Even making a pizza is too much for one person. I don't like leftovers, even though my husband loved leftovers. If I do make something, I'll take some to a friend. Try to share a meal with several people. My neighbors brought me pea soup, and I froze some for another meal. A bowl of chicken noodle soup and a salad is good." Mary B.

"Yes, my cooking changed. I find it hard to cook for one person. Sometimes I'll make dinner and have my daughter over. I'll go to the store where they have a 'hot bar' and get salmon or chicken, soup or a sandwich. You can always freeze food, but then you have to remember it's there." Lyn L.

"In the beginning, I didn't eat, and I lost weight. Then I got hungry. I would have a can of processed tuna or deli food. I've always enjoyed cooking, and now I still cook for two and take meals to friends, freeze, or share leftovers." Jolene M.

"I have no idea what advice to give to someone. If I eat out, I'll bring food home. I'll microwave TV dinners. For breakfast, I'll make regular oatmeal and add fruit or honey. I eat lots of fruit." Audrey C.

"I don't have a desire to cook for myself. When I eat out, I'll bring food home. That's an easy meal for the next day. I went to a restaurant and just ordered a chicken breast. Omaha Steaks has nice meals for two; I've fixed and eaten those for two days. If you have a steak in the freezer, you can make that and add a salad, potato, and vegetable. You can get delicious soups at Bob Evans and have enough for two to three days, adding something else to the meal like a salad. I'm getting out of the habit of buying something just because it's on sale. When I buy food, I'll put the new stuff behind the older stuff. I'm using up what I have in the freezer in the garage, trying to empty it. You have to remember you're not buying for two people anymore." Jan B.

And a final thought:

"It's hard cooking for one. You either overeat or you don't eat. In the beginning, I ate out too much because I didn't want to eat alone. Eat in front of the TV so you're not lonely. Sit down on Sunday and make a food plan with three recipes for the week. Two days per recipe equals six days of meals. I make one chicken recipe, one fish recipe like frozen cod, and one beef stew or chili. I use the Crock-Pot a lot. You can make spare ribs and add a vegetable and salad. Don't fall back on fast foods. Make nutritional choices." Evelyn C.

Ask yourself—

What are my immediate thoughts after reading this chapter on "Cooking and Eating for One"?

_____

_____

_____

_____

_____

Am I eating as nutritionally as I should be? If not, what could I do to remedy that?

_____

_____

_____

_____

_____

What ideas that I read sound as if they'd be easy for me to implement into my meal-planning?

_____

_____

_____

_____

What advice could I give with regard to easy, nutritional meals for one person?

_____

_____

_____

_____

What I want to remember from this chapter:

_____

_____

_____

_____

CHAPTER 15
Cleaning House

"What Am I Going to Do With All His Stuff?"

We were living in Florida when Pete passed, and I was left with his warm-climate wardrobe. I knew from talking with other women who were recently widowed how sad it had been for them to return and see their husband's clothes hanging in closets and folded in drawers. I knew I would shortly experience this when I returned to our northern home and didn't want to return to Florida in the fall and walk into our condo where Pete's personal items appeared to be waiting for him to walk through the door.

Deciding to ship most everything back to Wisconsin, where I could take my time sorting through it, I drove to the local grocery store and asked workers in the produce department for four large, sturdy apple boxes. Before I packed up the clothing to be mailed, there were a few items that Pete's brother Terry wanted and others that I gave to Pete's golf buddies. I donated a commode, safety grips for toilets, an assist bar for the bed, and bags of clothing to the thrift store run by our church; everything else would be shipped to Wisconsin in the apple boxes.

I chose to keep Pete's shaving kit, his favorite light jacket, his sunglasses, and a few other items at the condo. Why? It felt right to me at the time, and subconsciously, maybe I wanted something remaining in the condo to show he had once lived there with me. Like many widows whose husbands had been ill, I was left with numerous bottles of Pete's prescriptions, which, thankfully, the hospice nurses told me to bring in so they could dispose of them for me. (When I returned to Wisconsin, I took unused medications to the local police department, which had a disposal box for this purpose.)

The Florida apple boxes arrived shortly after I returned home. Our Wisconsin and out-of-state relatives, in town for the funeral, were invited to try on Pete's clothes and take what they could use. I could picture Pete smiling as my brother Greg did a reading at the funeral and looked so handsome wearing Pete's new navy blazer.

Even after the clothing distribution, there remained many of Pete's business clothes from his sales career. There were three-piece suits, sport jackets, dress shirts and slacks, ties, shoes, heavy winter overcoats, and lightweight spring trench coats, all of which I wanted to donate where they would be most appreciated. I went online and asked, "Where can I donate business clothes?" and discovered that not only does Men's Wearhouse hold an annual nation-wide clothing drive for gently used business clothing; their stores accept donations of this type of clothing throughout the year. Our local store was thrilled to accept my carload of Pete's business attire, and I knew Pete, looking down from above, loved knowing that his donated clothing was helping men enter the workforce or go on job interviews.

In the months that followed, still more clothing was taken to local charities, and Pete's extensive clothing inventory is slowly, but surely, being reduced. Of course there are drawers and closets that I still need to go through; there's a basement and garage filled with tools and everything else husbands like to collect that will need clearing out, but I'm in no hurry. I sold Pete's low-mileage, like-new 2014 Hyundai Azera to our nephew, who needed a dependable car for his family. What a great feeling knowing that the car Pete had so enjoyed driving was going to close relatives who would enjoy it as much as he had.

I would feel terrible if anyone reading this thought I coldheartedly was disposing of Pete's belongings when, in fact, my heart broke and my eyes filled with tears every time I sorted through his articles of clothing and remembered the times he had worn them. Then I would remind myself that Pete was always practical and would have wanted his belongings "being put to good use instead of just sitting there," as I could hear him saying.

You don't have to remove or go through your husband's belongings until you feel you're ready to do so, and, please, don't let anyone pressure you into doing anything you don't want to do.

You'll read in this chapter how women who have been widowed handled this delicate chore, and you'll see it's something that each widow does in her own way and in her own time.

"You have to be ready to give away his things. Some women do it right away, like purging. Some do it later. I went through my husband's things within a week. There were certain things I kept. I saved his pillow. I kept the clothes he was wearing when he passed away—the funeral home cleaned them. First, I asked his son what he wanted, and he took his dad's tools. There are so many homeless people who have nothing. I donated his things where they did the most good. He would be happy about that. One of the biggest causes of hoarding is unresolved grief, and that becomes toxic to you." Bobbi V.

"Don't be rushed. Do it when you're ready. You might go through things for an hour. It's easier to get rid of items you're not as attached to. I gave two of my husband's hats that didn't hold sentimental value to me to an assisted living facility." Beverly K.

"I gave his clothes to VA facilities in Wisconsin and Florida. They were so grateful and said sometimes they have to discharge vets, and they're not fully dressed. My husband's clothing went to people who needed them." Carol L.

"I did some sorting right away because my brothers and their wives were here for the funeral and helped me.

Within the last five years, I still had my husband's coats in the closet. I made my son go through them and pick out what he wanted. One of the coats went to my son's friend because it fit him. First, I asked people if they wanted anything and then donated the rest to charity and the church. Do it as soon as you can. I let it go because I was lazy, not sentimental. I kept his athletic socks because they fit me. My son wanted his dad's tools, but they're still in the garage because he hasn't taken them yet." Joanne W.

"I gave a lot of my husband's golf shirts to his friends. I kept a few things and gave others to his twin brother. I gave his watch to my former son-in-law, who had helped to take care of him. After a year, I sold his car. Other things I gave to charity. I still look at the jewelry in his jewelry box. I'm not going to keep his clothing in boxes to remind me of him. He's always in my heart." Ginny G.

"I went through his things within the first month or two. First, I put four of his favorite outfits to one side, and I still have them twenty years later. Then I offered what was left to family members. I gave his uniform to my stepson and then gave the rest to charity. With regard to furniture, I had to get rid of his recliner." Debbi C.

"I gave things to our sons and a lot to Goodwill and another charity." Shirley W.

"If something is meaningful to the family members, let them pick first, then donate or take the rest to a resale shop. Within a month, I got rid of his clothing. I asked relatives first, then took the rest to a resale shop. That first Christmas after he passed, my niece's husband came wearing one of my husband's shirts. It brought back memories, but I told him it looked good even though it really hit me to see him wearing it. I kept some of his jewelry, sold other pieces, and gave some to one of his cousins. I also kept one of his sweaters." Barb B.

"I'm still dealing with his things a year and a half later. You have to motivate yourself. Take your time. When you're ready, you'll do it. I'll end up giving a lot of his things to charities." Sandy G.

"I got rid of things relatively right away. Do it when you're ready. His clothing went to the Salvation Army. I went through the other stuff when I sold my house three and a half years later before I had an estate sale. The company that did the sale handled everything. I gave his tools to the son of a friend, who was so grateful. I did keep a little toolbox so I'd have some tools if I needed them." Barb W.

"My husband died in January. Homeless people on the streets were cold. My sister helped me take 99 percent of his clothing to the Rescue Mission. I kept some of his things and did give a few things to other people." Kay P.

"The hospice where he died accepted his clothes to put in their thrift store." Ruby C.

"I did this soon after he passed. I donated a lot of his clothes to various charities. His tools were donated to Habitat for Humanity, where they'll be used to build houses.

They even came to pick up the tools and were so grateful to get them. I sold his golf clubs. He had a commemorative jacket. I took a picture of the emblem on it and then gave it away. I'll give his watch to our grandson when he graduates from high school. When I was getting ready to sell my house, to move into a condo, there were three groups of things I had to get rid of, and this might help someone moving. First, throw out anything that's broken. The second group's a little harder but not much—tools and things you can donate. The third group is the hardest—the sentimental things like ornaments, nativity sets. Whatever the family didn't take had to go. I put some things on a neighborhood website. In spring, college kids setting up their first apartments bought the furniture. You want to get rid of the stuff, so price it to sell. Be aware of scams. I had put some furniture on Craigslist. A guy called and said he was interested in my dining room set but wanted me to pay the shipping to send it to him. My reply was 'I don't think so!'" Lila S.

"My husband passed away while he was in an assisted living facility, so I had to clear out his things right away. I gave his things to the Salvation Army, including his assist aids. My daughters removed a lot of his stuff for me. His hobby was genealogy research, and I still have all those papers relating to that to go through." Audrey C.

"Soon after he passed, I went through his things. The kids took some, and I gave a lot to Goodwill. His tools went to Habitat for Humanity. I was moving and had to purge. Some women make being a widow into a drama and keep their husband's things. I didn't do that. Someone told me to keep his robe because it would have his smell on it, but it didn't. I kept some of his cuff links and gloves." Pearl G.

"I immediately went through his things. My husband had a fit when he saw his brother-in-law had kept his wife's things for over a year. He told me never to do that with his. Our sons got what they wanted, and I donated a lot. There were some things I kept. His wedding ring will go to one of the grandsons if he wants it. I gave his casual clothes to the grooms at the stable where I kept my horse, and they were so grateful." Angie O.

"Two and a half years later, I still have almost all his clothes. I gave some of his sweat shirts to our granddaughter and some of his jewelry to my stepchildren. I'm keeping some of his tools and leaving the rest for his son. My husband had large feet, so I told the college if there were any football players who needed large shoes, they could have them." Joyce B.

"I didn't have to think about getting rid of his things. My brothers took all the clothes and stuff home with them. My sons wanted the lawnmower and snowblower. I kept his coat." Kathy H.

"Someone told me to get rid of my husband's things in one week. I loaded everything—clothes, golf clubs, shoeshine kit—into my car and drove to my stepdaughter's home. I told her to look through everything and take whatever she wanted. Then I drove to my stepson's house and did the same thing. I kept my husband's robe and a couple of his shirts. I took the rest of his clothes to a church sale when I went back to Ohio. Personally, I don't think you should donate your husband's clothes to a charity in your town. I didn't want to see a homeless person wearing my husband's clothes." Lee M.

"It's very hard to do. I started about two months after he passed. First, I asked the kids, and they took what they wanted. Then I started packing what was left. I kept a flannel shirt he wore and his wallet." Nancy J.

"I went through his things when it was convenient for me. I gave many things to my handyman, who has done so much for me and the family, and took other things to the hospital resale. My daughter helped the first time I went through his things. I gave some to organizations who help men trying to get established in the workforce. I kept his favorite sweater." Kay J.

"After about a month, I donated most of his clothes to the Salvation Army. Some of his baseball (golf) caps I kept for my grandsons. I kept some of his T-shirts to sleep in." Judie N.

"Do it little by little. In less than six months, I gave stuff to my brother-in-law and friends. A lot I gave to charity." Marijo Z.

"We lived on an island outside of New York, and after four months, I gave his tools to the Mexican workers there who had families to feed. They were so appreciative. His golf stuff went to our son and his clothes to Goodwill." Evelyn C.

"Don't give yourself a timeline to give his things away. Twelve years later I still have some of my husband's things. Our two sons took some, and I'm still taking things to charities." Carole C.

"I gave his personal belongings to each of his children. If the one I gave something to didn't want it, they could give it to the other. As I'm going through his office in Michigan, if I find something of personal interest to his children, I'll put that aside. I gave some articles of his clothing and some appliances to a charity, House by the Side of the Road, run by our church in Michigan. Homeless people who can't pay for things go there." Gladi B.

"I still have quite a bit of his clothing. I started going through his pants and gave them to the Salvation Army. A neighbor came around recently collecting men's clothing for his church to give to the needy. I gave them a lot of his clothing, and they were so happy to get the donation. I want someone to get use out of his things." Jan B.

"After about two to three months, I took a lot of his things to Goodwill." Joan A.

"I did it within six months. I gave most of his clothes to Goodwill. Those clothes that still had tags on, I took back to the stores, and they gave me credit. I kept some of his special things like from sports teams. Many hospices have volunteers who will make a Care Bear out of special pieces of clothing." Lyn L.

"I did nothing until it felt right. There was no rush. Most of his things were in Minnesota, a few were at our condo in Florida. He passed in October, and I knew he would want his winter coats to go to those who needed them. I gave his golf clubs and tools to his buddies. I wanted his things to go to the kind of 'home' that seemed right. I used his T-shirts for sleeping or lounging or cut them down for work-out clothes." Jolene M.

And a final thought:

"Remember, all decisions are yours in dispensing your husband's belongings. I started going through his things fairly quickly, about a month after he passed. I did it mostly for our cat Haley, who would go into his clothes closet, pull his clothes down, and sit on them. She was much better after his things were gone. Our son's wedding ring had cracked, so I gave him his dad's. He still wears it. The day of the funeral, I let my sons pick out pieces of jewelry that they wanted. Surprisingly, each chose what I would have predicted they would. I gave many of his things to a close friend who was the same size and a lot to the hospital resale shop because they had done so much for him." Mary B.

Ask yourself—

After reading this chapter on "Cleaning House," what are some of my immediate thoughts?

_____

_____

_____

_____

_____

Personal things of my husband's that I would like to keep are:

_____

_____

_____

_____

Who do I think would appreciate articles of his clothing, jewelry, his tools?

_____

_____

_____

_____

What ideas did I get from this chapter?

_____

_____

_____

_____

_____

What advice would I give to someone regarding her husband's belongings?

_____

_____

_____

_____

_____

What I want to remember from this chapter:

_____

_____

_____

_____

_____

CHAPTER 16
Household Chores

Use Your Ingenuity to Get Things Done

Your husband is gone, but the chores or repairs he may have taken care of around the house, condo, apartment—wherever you're living—are still going to be there. If you live in an apartment, you'll usually have a maintenance person to take care of any repairs. You won't need to mow the lawn or remove snow from the driveway, but now you're the person who will have to complain to the manager when the faucet is leaking, the lawn is beginning to look like a field, or the snow is piling up. You'll need to take decisive action to be sure the jobs you're paying for are getting done. Be polite but firm. Don't let anyone attempt to take advantage of you because you're a widow, and, yes, "widow bullies" do exist. If you live in a condo, outside maintenance will be included in your association fees.

If you're a homeowner and your husband was required to travel, unable to do chores, or simply didn't care to do them, you may have done many things around the house yourself or already have a system in place to deal with the upkeep of your home. For example, the lawn service Pete hired years ago when his health began to fail still takes care of our property.

If, however, your husband was doing the repairs or chores when he passed, taking charge of these has become your responsibility, and you need a game plan. That means if you can fix or do it yourself, do so; if not, don't be afraid to ask for help or hire someone if you can afford it.

If a lightbulb burns out, do you have a spare bulb handy? If the bulb that needs replacing is too high for you to reach, are there relatives or neighbors nearby whom you can ask for help? Always remember, you never want to be in a situation where you could fall and injure yourself. Two lightbulbs located high inside my garage burned out, and Jim, my across-the-driveway neighbor, was kind enough to replace them for me. He also keeps a lookout for any outside garage lights that may need replacing when I'm away. Jim and his wife Lana even helped carry old screen and patio doors, too heavy for one person to lift, up from the basement.

Although I'm blessed with caring neighbors, as I've mentioned earlier in this book, a reputable handyman who charges a reasonable price for his work is worth his weight in gold. Ask family or friends for referrals or go onto a neighborhood website. After my Wisconsin handyman Mike had replaced the outside dryer vent and cleaned out the dryer hose in the basement, he asked when I had last put salt in the water softener. I'm sure I had a "deer in the headlights" look on my face because that was the last thing on my mind during the past year of Pete's doctor appointments, treatments, hospitalizations, and rehab stays. Mike purchased six bags of salt, dumped three into the bone-dry water softener, and stacked the other bags where they'd be handy for future use. Now, on the advice of my neighbor Jim, I have the company that installed our water softener deliver the bags of salt for the cost of each bag, which is around $9.95. With Mike or his dad Gene on call, I needn't ask my neighbors or family members every time I need something done. When I'm in Florida, I have my handyman Al to take care of things in the condo. He had installed and repaired things when Pete was alive and said he's always there to help me when I need it.

I've phoned our service provider when I couldn't get the TV to work, and the techs walked me through the rebooting process. When I finally had a picture on the screen, that was definitely a "Yay! I fixed it" moment. I wrote down everything they told me to do so I can try to fix it without calling them immediately if it happens again. The printer in the office stopped working, so I needed to purchase a new one, which my friend Sue installed for me. I've replaced the printer ink cartridges by following directions I found online.

After two large trees fell during a storm and destroyed our shed in the backyard, my next-door neighbor Mike (not "handyman Mike") came over to offer condolences on Pete's passing and asked if I needed help with anything. I asked if he knew anyone who could take down what remained of the shed, and Mike said he loved "to destroy stuff!" He went home, returned with his chainsaw, and dismantled what remained of the shed, burning much of the scrap in his fire-pit.

The shed contained our old riding lawn mower but was mostly packed with stuff accumulated over the years. My cousin Marilyn had stopped over to see how I was doing, and while Mike worked on the demolition, she and I loaded the useless items onto a tarp, dragged it across the lawn, and piled everything in the driveway for the garbage men. I wasn't too proud to ask for or accept help, and people were glad to come to my aid because it was something they could do for me.

I'm including car maintenance in this chapter, and you may be fortunate to have a friend or family member who knows cars and has offered to take care of yours. That's wonderful, but if you don't have a "car person" looking out for you, here are a few good tips to follow. Pete loved cars and always said the least expensive car maintenance was to get regular oil changes, something which is easy for you to do. Make sure you never run out of gas; I top off the tank when I see the gas gauge at the halfway mark. If your car doesn't feel or sound right or a dashboard alert light goes on, take the car into a reputable dealer or auto body shop recommended by friends or family. Putting off car repairs will only create more problems, and you don't want to find yourself stranded on the side of a road, especially at night.

Women who have been widowed have many suggestions for taking care of those household chores and repairs now that you're on your own.

"My husband traveled a lot, and his heart was weakened, so I did many chores around the house. If you don't know how to do stuff, you'll have to learn or ask. Make a schedule on a calendar for dates when you'll change the water softener salt, have the furnace checked, change the filter on the ice maker, have the oil changed in the car, have the lawn mower checked before spring. A great gift for a new widow is a toolbox." Barb W.

"I fix a lot of things around the house myself. I've fixed several toilets. After seeing how things were put together, I just fixed them. If it's something I can't do, I'll ask a friend to do it or get a referral from someone I know. My grandson does my lawn, and I pay him. My neighbor plows for me." Kay P.

"My husband traveled for work, so I did a lot around the house myself, including the windows. Four years before he passed, we had started replacing the windows with double-hung windows so I didn't have to bother with screens. I also mowed the lawn and snow-blowed the driveway. I also did all the painting around the house." Debbi C.

"Jump into it. You might feel lost at first. Ask, 'How do I run the lawnmower?' Ask a professional if you need help. Say, 'I've never done this before. How do I do it?' There are always how-to-do-it books for you to read." Bobbi V.

"You may not anticipate that you'll need tools, but you will. Get yourself a toolbox and put tools in it. I had my own toolbox, but my husband and son took things out of it and didn't put them back. Make sure to keep a hammer, pliers, wrenches, and screwdrivers. Keep some tools, especially if you have a house. You're not as helpless as you may think you are. I have a lawn and driveway guy, a guy who does remodeling, a guy who does windows, and a handyman. The hardest thing about owning a home and being alone is decision-making. In the beginning, I didn't have a clue on what to do." Joanne W.

"When I'm in Florida, I'll call my son-in-law. When I'm at my house in New York, I have a cleaning woman and a lawn service. If something goes out in the house, I'll call service people. My sons are nearby and are handy." Audrey C.

"You have to speak up for yourself. When I was talking to the insurance company, instead of answering my questions, the girl told me to go online. I talked to the manager, who told me whom to talk to the next time I called. When I moved into my condo, I hung most of my own pictures, and a friend helped with a few things. I'd rather hire a handyman because then you're not beholden to someone. Fire and smoke detectors are hard to reach when you have high ceilings, so I installed five-year batteries and put stickers on them saying when they'll need to be replaced." Pearl G.

"I live in a single-family house in my complex, so I don't have to do anything outside; the homeowners association dues take care of that. I have the names of handymen for other jobs." Jan B.

"We had a handyman who did it all, and I kept him. The lawn service, driveway, and repairs are all taken care of." Kathy H.

"If the snow is under three inches and not heavy or wet, I'll take care of it. Otherwise, I have someone to plow the driveway. I have a lawn service but do a lot of things myself." Ginny G.

"Hire a good handyman. I have an upstairs tenant in my duplex who does some chores for me like shoveling the driveway." Shirley W.

"If it's a project like clearing the leaves, one of my sons helps me blow and collect them. All my kids help me. They helped me paint the kitchen. One of my sons is my 'worker.'" Nancy J.

"My husband had helped with half the cleaning. Now I do it all. For the house in Minnesota, I bought a home warranty for an annual fee of $400.00 and $75.00 service calls. It was a great move. They'll send someone out to fix a stopped sink, electrical problem, a sewer backup caused by tree roots." Jolene M.

"If it's something I can't do myself, I'll call a handyman." Ruby C.

"I used to take care of everything in the house while he took care of the business. I have a good handyman, and I'll take him with me, for instance, when I go to talk about putting in a new driveway." Kay J.

"If you can take care of it yourself, deal with it. Otherwise, get a good handyman." Beverly K.

"Get a person to do jobs you don't want to do or can't do yourself. Always have a good handyman. Mine will come out when I have a half day's work. He charges by the hour, $75.00 for two men to work. I don't want to hurt my back, so I have a cleaning lady once a month. She even gets on a ladder to clean the ceiling fans. I had always done pretty much everything around the house." Lee M.

"I live in a condo, so the association does all the repairs. I have a person to check on things when I'm not there." Carol L.

"My husband taught me how to fix things mechanically, so I manage to fix a lot in the house I share with my daughter. I do my own lawn care and snowplowing. I have a handyman service. My daughter and I make up a 'honey-do' list because it's $200.00 for someone to come out, and we want to make sure we have a lot for him to do. My nephews and brother-in-law will help if it's something I can't do, and they'll give me information." Lou H.

"I do my own cleaning but hire someone to do the windows." Judie N.

"I sold my home, and now I'm renting a house. I have to keep calling to get things done. Don't be afraid to ask for help. Talk to neighbors and get references. Don't call 'blind' from ads. I have a great car dealership that takes care of my car." Marijo Z.

"I have a sturdy stepladder. Don't get on a big ladder. I wash my own windows, clean my car, and sweep the garage. The owners of the house I rent have service people if I need them. I do as much as I safely can because it's good for my mind. I wash smaller loads of wash than before. My sons come down, and I know they're checking on me." Angie O.

"My two sons help me with household chores. If it's something they can't fix, I'll hire someone." Carole C.

"Get someone to cut the grass. My daughter's father-in-law helped me a lot. I had a plumbing problem and had to get the plumber back to fix it. I worry about air in the tires and things like that." Sandy G.

"After my first husband died, I did all my own chores. I shoveled the driveway and mowed the lawn. I never had a cleaning lady in the twenty-eight years between my first husband's passing and my marriage to my second husband." Gladi B.

"I do what I can and hire a handyman for the things I can't do." Joan A.

"Having a good, trustworthy handyman is important. My next-door neighbor does stuff for me. He won't take money but likes Bud Light beer. I buy him a case every two months to thank him for what he does, and he's happy. All my neighbors are helpful; one was a licensed plumber, which comes in handy." Mary B.

"I have way less to do because I moved to a condo. You can hire experts for the big things, but the little things are hardest, for example, changing a lightbulb in the ceiling or putting on a license plate. I can't always call my son; he has three children who keep him busy." Lila S.

"You can hire a handyman to do a lot of things. Because I'm in a condo, I don't have to do the lawn or driveway. I do the wash once a week." Barb B.

"I do the wash as needed, and many of the things I let air-dry. The linens get changed on Sunday. I always took the garbage out the night before pickup. I have someone to plow the driveway. Now I complain if it's not done the way it should be. I used to not complain, but now I'm paying for it and want it done right. When I went to buy some new appliances, the saleslady said to replace them all. I said, 'Are you going to pay for it?' She was taken aback." Lyn L.

"It was a difficult day for me when I was doing the laundry and realized I wouldn't have his things to fold anymore. That hit me hard. I have a lot of good people to rely on. Ask for help when you need it. You may hate to do that, but you have to get used to it." Evelyn C.

And a final thought:

"I don't do the wash as often now that it's just me. The same kid does my lawn and driveway. Find a good handyman recommended by friends or family or from a neighborhood website. Find a good mechanic that you can trust.

That's very important. I top off the gas tank when it gets down to half. I hate Thursdays because now I have to take out the garbage. If anyone wants to help a widow, ask when the garbage is picked up and take it out for her. The light in my shower burned out. I got a sturdy stepstool, put a cloth under it to keep it from slipping, and changed the bulb. My daughter said I had to learn how to do things. I told her, 'Not everything.'" Joyce B.

Ask yourself—

What were my immediate thoughts after reading the chapter on "Household Chores"?

_____

_____

_____

_____

_____

Some of my household chores that would require outside help include:

_____

_____

_____

_____

_____

Where would I get help with these chores when I need it?

_____

_____

_____

_____

_____

What advice would I give to someone who asked for suggestions as to whom she could call for outside help around the house?

_____

_____

_____

_____

_____

What I want to remember from this chapter:

_____

_____

_____

_____

_____

CHAPTER 17
The Bedroom

Sleeping Habits, Sheets, & That Empty Side

When you're a wife, the bedroom is a place of intimacy and meant to be shared by you and your husband. It's a room where the two of you love, talk, laugh, and create many beautiful memories. Then your husband is gone, and the bedroom is yours alone.

For many of you, your husband's framed picture is on the nightstand; it's what you see when you open your eyes in the morning and before you close them at night. As I mentioned in a previous chapter, every morning I look at Pete's picture and say, "Good morning, sweetheart! Love you! Start the day!" just as we always said to one another. At night I still say, "Night, sweetheart. Love you." That was our routine for forty-four years, and it's comforting for me to continue it.

My sleep patterns drastically changed after Pete passed. I still slept on my side of the bed, but I no longer fell asleep as soon as my head hit the pillow or slept soundly throughout the night. There were many nights when I would lie awake, listening to my two cats purring on either side of me. Other women who've been widowed told me the sleeplessness I was experiencing would pass. However, after eight months of sleepless nights, I told my doctor about my problem, and she prescribed a sleeping aid. At bedtime, I take one-quarter of a pill, which works perfectly. Finally, I'm sleeping again.

I dearly miss being able to curl up and spoon with Pete or to snuggle with my "human furnace," as I'd call him, on chilly nights. When he was in the hospital or rehab, sometimes he'd ask me to join him in his bed, and we'd take a nap together. I remember one of the CNAs exclaiming, "Oh, they're so cute!" when she came into his room and saw us. Perhaps my sleeplessness was because subconsciously I knew he wasn't where I'd be able to visit him in the morning, that he wasn't physically here any longer. I've since read that insomnia is a reaction to loss, something I found very interesting.

I miss not having Pete help me make the bed or check my "military corners," which were never as perfect as his. Now, instead of completely removing the heavy comforter at night, I'll fold my half over Pete's side of the bed. One of my widowed friends told me she knows someone who alternates sleeping on either side of the bed to use both sides of the sheets. If you don't want to do that, you can achieve the same results by switching the bottom of the sheets to the top every other time you change them.

How women who have been widowed deal with bedroom issues is interesting and may strike some familiar chords with you:

"In the beginning, I had a long body pillow, and using it felt like he was there. I still use it. I also sleep on two pillows and hug the small one. I went from a king-size bed to a queen. I use a beautiful woven wool bedspread that was ours. It reverses for summer and winter. My bedroom has many good memories. In the beginning, I had trouble sleeping, and when that happened, I would read or pace. Now I sleep." Barb B.

"I sleep on one side of the bed one week and on the other side the next week. Then I don't have to undo the bedding for two weeks. I kept thinking I would get a smaller bed, but then what would I do with the old bed and bedding?" Jan B.

"Keeping the TV on in the bedroom helps. If you're having trouble sleeping in the bedroom, fall asleep watching TV. Meditation helps, and there are tapes to help you get to sleep. Go to the doctor for a sleeping med if you need it." Marijo Z.

"I'll put pillows on his side of the bed so it looks like someone is sleeping there. I'll also switch bedrooms. Sometimes I'll fall asleep on the couch. Sleeping is overrated." Ruby C.

"I have two sets of sheets to rotate and still sleep on my side of the bed. I'll turn the mattress around to change sides, not turn it upside down because it's too heavy. I sleep with the TV on all night like my husband and I did." Lyn L.

"I touch his picture. I'll move all the pillows to his side and touch them. I'll sleep on his side of the bed. If I can't sleep, I'll listen to NPR on the radio." Sandy G.

"I have both of my husbands' pictures next to my bed and say good night to each and tell each that I love him." Gladi B.

"I had a Native American 'smudging' ceremony to get the negative energy out of the room and rearranged the furniture. I couldn't sleep soundly for over a year; I slept in the guest room. I'll make half the bed." Evelyn C.

"I have a king mattress, so I sleep on both sides. It's annoying to change king sheets, so then I only have to do it every two weeks." Pearl G.

"My husband had been more comfortable sleeping in a chair, so I was already sleeping alone. Now I have my dog sleeping with me." Judie N.

"I still have some sleepless nights, but I have sleep apnea. I sleep on my side of the bed and changed from our king-size bed to a full size." Lou H.

"I had trouble sleeping before my husband passed because he had heart problems, and I kept listening to him breathing. I sleep on my side of the bed; the other side is still his side." Carol L.

"I hate the king-size bed. I can't sleep on the side where he died and sleep on the other side. At first, I had trouble sleeping and would be waking up all night. I'd turn on the TV, which helped because it keeps your mind from thinking, and then I'd fall asleep. Now I might have some trouble sleeping but not as much. It helps to do something physical so your body is tired. Remember, too, as we get older, we don't sleep as well. It's a human condition." Kay J.

"I'll say good night to him. I sleep in the nude and all over the bed, not on one side." Audrey C.

"After he died, I slept on my side of the bed." Debbi C.

"When my husband, who had Parkinson's disease, became very ill, he couldn't sleep with me in the bed anymore, and that broke my heart. When we had slept together, I would wrap his T-shirt around my hand so I would know if he tried to get out of bed. His balance was bad, and he had fallen and broken his back three times. Now I'm more afraid at night when I hear noises. I didn't sleep well when I tried sleeping on his side of the bed. I don't like sleeping alone." Lee M.

"I've never been a good sleeper, so my husband's passing didn't affect my sleep habits. I just felt relief that he was at peace." Shirley W.

"I had trouble sleeping and hated to go to bed because we had always gone to bed together. I sleep on my own side, and my cat Haley sleeps on my husband's side." Mary B.

"I turned the mattress over myself. I place his pillow behind me to feel like he's there." Jolene M.

"Because of his illness, my husband was more comfortable sleeping in a chair, so I was used to sleeping alone." Joan A.

"I had trouble sleeping for over a year. I'd hear noises or the house creaking. I sleep on his side of the bed and put a pillow behind me so it feels like he's behind me." Nancy J.

"Until last year, fourteen years after he passed, I could only sleep on my side of the bed, never on his side. Now I can sleep on both sides." Ginny G.

"My bedroom was a safe place for me. I couldn't sleep and went to the doctor, who said I had to rest. I took Ambien for three months. Then I went off the drug and took half a Benadryl, which put me to sleep." Kathy H.

"I slept soundly after he passed, but I sleep on my side of the bed." Lila S.

"Three days after my husband died, I bought a body pillow because I was cold and wanted something behind me. Now I keep ankle socks near the bed in case my feet get cold. The first week after he died, I slept so soundly; I hadn't realized how exhausted I was. I started menopause, had night sweats, wasn't sleeping, and asked my doctor for something. He gave me an estrogen gel, which really helped, and also a low dose of an antidepressant. Don't be afraid to ask your doctor for a sleeping aid or an antidepressant." Joyce B.

"I sleep on my side of the bed." Beverly K.

"I still have trouble sleeping ten years after my husband passed. If I can't sleep, I'll get up and play solitaire on the computer, or I'll read and then go back to bed. I still sleep on my side of the bed because the other side is still his side. I used to fold the bedspread over half of the bed. Now my dog and the dogs I'm taking care of sleep there." Angie O.

"I slept on my own side at first, then switched to his side, then to the middle. The first year I said good night to him and talked to him before bed." Barb W.

"I either sleep on my own side of the bed, or I'll sleep diagonally. The week of the funeral, I had trouble sleeping because I had company staying with me, and I was worrying about what I would say when I addressed the people at the luncheon following the funeral. I was still working during the day, so my mind was occupied." Joanne W.

"You have trouble sleeping in the beginning because you're thinking about things. We had a king-size bed, and I recently sold it and bought a queen size. If, eventually, I would move to an apartment, most aren't big enough for a king. I'll turn the sheets around so both sides get used. If I can't sleep, I'll use melatonin or an over-the-counter sleep aid. I can't read books too late at night, so reading magazines with short articles like '*Reader's Digest* works for me." Kay P.

And a final thought:

"To go from his being with you to his not being there is part of the work from grief to healing. I was used to sleeping alone because our jobs often kept us from sleeping together. I slept with his pillow and T-shirt. His scent was calming. My kitties were always there in bed with me and that helped." Bobbi V.

Ask yourself—

After reading this chapter "The Bedroom," what are my immediate thoughts?

_____

_____

_____

_____

_____

I could relate to the women with regard to:

_____

_____

_____

_____

_____

The advice or information that I found most interesting or comforting and would share with someone newly widowed was:

_____

_____

_____

_____

_____

What I want to remember from this chapter:

_____

_____

_____

_____

_____

CHAPTER 18
Be Prepared

It Will Make Your Life So Much Easier

This chapter is going to branch off in various directions. We have many ideas to prepare you for different circumstances that may arise now that you're on your own.

For the first five months after Pete passed, I carried a copy of his death certificate in my purse, never knowing when I might be asked to produce it while cancelling accounts or switching accounts over to my name. Just when I decided I probably wouldn't need to have it with me, I was asked for it at my bank when I switched from a regular to a Money Market savings account. Having a copy of the death certificate saved me a trip home to retrieve it. There's now a copy in the glove compartment of my car.

Be sure you know your husband's account numbers for charge accounts, banking and investment accounts, all insurances, any car loans, utility companies, phone provider, and his social security number. Keep these account numbers handy, preferably in one place, so if you're cancelling or switching accounts over to your name as primary account holder, you won't be wasting time trying to track them down. I keep these, along with user names and passwords, in a small notebook available at most bookstores or office supply stores. Obviously, you're not going to carry this notebook filled with confidential information in your purse but will store it in a safe place.

A phone charger that plugs into the charger in your car is good to have, especially if you're using GPS, which quickly runs down a cell phone's battery. With a charger, you won't have to worry about losing battery power on your phone. You needn't keep the charger plugged in constantly, but it's reassuring to know it's there if your phone begins to lose power.

Pete always kept a hundred-dollar bill folded in a compartment in his wallet. When Pete was a young man, an elderly friend of his suggested he do that so he'd always have "emergency" money. I don't keep a hundred dollars, but there is a twenty-dollar bill folded in my wallet "just in case."

As I said in an earlier chapter, my car's gas tank gets topped off when the gauge drops to the halfway mark. I certainly don't want to be caught in a traffic jam or stranded somewhere with an empty gas tank.

At home I keep a spare key hidden outside so I don't have to call a locksmith if I accidentally lock myself out. My spare key also comes in handy if I need someone to get inside the house for any number of reasons. It's a good investment.

In my wallet I keep a list of prescriptions, their doses, and reasons for taking them. I also keep a list of past surgeries with the dates they occurred. Both lists have been useful while filling out forms in doctors' offices or when I've been asked questions by medical personnel. My phone contains not only my doctors' phone numbers but also their fax numbers and addresses. If you don't own a smartphone, make a list to keep in your wallet. Yes, that wallet may become a little thick, but this is all important information. Be sure to change emergency contacts in your phone and other places like doctors' offices. Have a list of people for your family to notify if something happens to you. You could use a Christmas card list or your address book.

Being prepared for situations that arise is something women who have been widowed have experience with, and these are their suggestions:

"Never be afraid to ask for help. Pace yourself. It's okay to say no to things if you don't feel up to it. Be prepared for good days and bad days. Take things moment to moment." Debbi C.

"Be really organized! I use file folders and pocket folders. I have a little metal stand next to the computer for the two to three folders I need more often at certain times, so they're easily accessible. Don't save what you don't need. Shred any unneeded material. Many banks will do it free of charge." Lyn L.

"I just had my will redone. I told the kids to go through the house, and I'll mark what they want when I'm gone.

They didn't want to talk about it, but I said it was good to do. There was only one thing that more than one of them wanted. They can draw cards or throw dice to see who gets it." Nancy J.

"I kept some basic tools and bought a set of tools at Ace Hardware." Joanne W.

"I have my husband's death certificate in the back of my calendar. Be very organized! Use files in a file drawer. Use labels. Keep 'your ducks in a row.'" Kathy H.

"Unexpected things will come up. For example, we had a dual listing in the phone book. Now I'm getting mail in his name. It's good I had many copies of his death certificate. When I got a call from a phone provider for an outstanding bill, I told the company they had never been my provider and that my husband had been deceased for many years. I said someone may have given our phone number to the company, but we had never had an account with them." Barb B.

"Keep up with car repairs. If a light goes on, get it checked." Carol L.

"You're alone. The first time you get sick, you think, *I could die, and no one would know for a while.* My neighbor asked for a key so she's able to check on me. If you misplace or lose your car keys often, there's no one to call. A friend gave me an elastic band key holder. One end attaches to the inside of your purse and the other to your keys. Join AAA (American Automobile Association) or have an insurance policy where you can call them if you get a flat tire or your car stalls. Make a list of repair people. Have it ready before you need it because you want to be able to get to it in a hurry. Get recommendations from friends and family. Get the name of a good handyman." Barb W.

"Get regular oil changes for your car. When they change the oil, they'll check the car. I have a death certificate with me just in case I need it." Kay P.

"If I needed something, I could go to my church. There are twenty-four deacons who minister to those who need help. The church even has mechanics who volunteer twice a month to do oil changes for people, like widows." Beverly K.

"I didn't expect I'd have to send a death certificate to the water company to change the account over to my name. You can't really be prepared for everything that comes up." Judie N.

"With regard to your car repairs, you're at their (mechanics) mercy. If I think something is wrong with the car, I'll take it in. My sons helped me understand more when I took the car in for work. I have good neighbors and good friends to help me. Don't be ashamed to tell people you trust that you don't know about something." Angie O.

"My advice is to use common sense. Make as many of your own decisions as you can. I was brought up to make decisions and to do things myself. If you need help, ask a family member or friend." Shirley W.

"You need someone you can talk to about things, some-one who won't have anything to gain from whatever you're asking them about. Have a good financial advisor. Never have anyone as executor for your estate who has something to gain from it. Don't have a family member as executor because that can cause friction between family members." Lee M.

"I'm still learning every day. My husband used to put gas in the tank; now I'm the one who does it. I'll go to the car wash to wash my car." Ginny G.

"I still have a copy of his death certificate in my glove compartment in case I need it. If you go somewhere, take your own car. Practice how you're going to explain your husband's death. I say, 'I'm married, but my husband is in Heaven.' If there's a form without a place to check 'widow,' I check 'married.' In our culture, 'widow' has a negative con-notation like 'a helpless person' or 'black widow.' I'm not lonely. I just miss my husband." Joyce B.

"My kids ordered copies of his death certificate for me to use when I change accounts over to my name." Kay P.

"Watch the gas gauge in your car. Be sure the car is tak-en care of. Don't drive in bad weather. At first, I had AAA to help if something happened with the car. Now my insur-ance company will send someone if my car has a problem. My water softener company will put salt in the tank. They'll send me an email to remind me when it's time." Lou H.

"There are a lot of surprises you can't be prepared for. Talk to friends for advice." Ruby C.

"Fill the gas tank when the gauge is moving towards one-quarter full. Pay attention always. Have a reliable place to take your car. Ask friends and relatives for advice as to where to go. Getting regular oil changes and checking your tires are very important. I go to where I bought my car because they were friends of my husband. Dealers may charge more money, but they have a history of the car. If you weren't before, you are now the person responsible for your car." Joanne W.

"I keep a calendar where I write down where I have to be. I also keep a log on what I did. Write down car repairs (ex. when you changed the oil or filters), household maintenance (ex. when the furnace was serviced)." Evelyn C.

"I'm going to go to the memorial gardens where my husband and I bought our crypt years ago to make my funeral arrangements and get details on cremation." Mary B.

"Don't make decisions on the run. Think them through. Have someone trustworthy you can ask for advice." Joan A.

"If an appliance goes down, you need to decide if you want to repair or replace it. Look at its age and ask yourself that question." Jan B.

"Check your fuel gauge. When I had a Cessna plane (I was a pilot), I would use a tall ladder to reach the fuel tank and fill it myself. Now my kids fill my gas tank when I need it. I have a coded lock on the door of my condo, so I don't need a key. I always put the deadbolt on at night. My kids take care of a lot for me." Audrey C.

"Be prepared that grief will hit you. When I returned to Florida, I could not drive into the condo building's parking lot. On Christmas morning, I took my friend's dog to the beach where my husband and I used to go. My dog rushed up to another dog, and the owner and I talked. When I asked her the dog's name, she said it was Jolene (my name). I burst into tears because it seemed my husband was near me." Jolene M.

"Be sure you know where to find your copies of his death certificates. Keep his Social Security card where you can find it. Social Security rears its head every so often. I haven't thrown out all the funeral cards yet, but I'm going to get rid of most of them. Then the kids won't have to do it." Pearl G.

And a final thought:

"There will be things that you can't resolve yourself and then you'll need a professional. You might have to raise hell to get something done. If you're not a strong person who's able to fight for something, think of someone you know who's strong and assume that person's persona. You can also ask yourself what your husband or the strongest person you know would do. Be prepared to find out who your friends are. You might have to eliminate some people from your circle of friends. There are those people who want to have power over you, and you're currently in a weakened state. Be careful of those who think they know what you need more than you do." Bobbi V.

Ask yourself—

After reading this chapter "Be Prepared," what are some of my immediate thoughts?

_____

_____

_____

_____

_____

Some things I hadn't thought of before were:

_____

_____

_____

_____

_____

This is what I'm going to do to prepare for those things I hadn't considered before:

_____

_____

_____

_____

_____

Advice on the subject of being prepared that I would give to another woman would be:

_____

_____

_____

_____

_____

What I want to remember from this chapter:

_____

_____

_____

_____

_____

CHAPTER 19
Social Invitations
Think Before Declining Them

How you respond to social invitations is going to depend on several factors: who is inviting you, where you'll be going, and what you'll be doing. We're not necessarily referring to events that involve couples; that will be covered in the next chapter. The social invitations we're discussing here are those where you've been invited to attend events that get you out of the house.

A friend was told to accept every invitation unless she was ill or had another commitment because if she turned down too many, people would eventually stop inviting her. She's followed that advice and is glad she did. The alternative was for her to stay home, concentrate on her loss, and feel sorry for herself. She was a social person before her husband passed, and her personality hasn't changed.

My girlfriends continue to ask me to join them for lunch, movies, or shopping, and I accept their invitations. I also call them to set up get-togethers. Remember, don't always wait for others to do the calling; you need to do your share of calling, as well.

After Pete passed, I was invited places by friends who had known us for years and wanted to be there for me. I felt comfortable with these long-time friends and wanted to be there for them, as well. That's something we need to keep reminding ourselves; we're not the only ones grieving our loss. Pete had so many friends, and even though they knew he was very ill, his death still came as a shock to friends, family, and neighbors in Wisconsin who hadn't witnessed his rapidly deteriorating health in those last months in Florida. By including me in social events, I became, in a sense, their connection to Pete. There may not have been a "Pete and Bonnie" to invite any longer, but there was still a "Bonnie." I've been invited to house parties, movies, plays, and events at the various clubs to which I still belong.

These were events that had been put on hold, especially during the last year, when Pete's physical condition depleted so much of his energy. He and I had always been a very social couple, and it was difficult for Pete to be forced to turn down invitations when he was too tired or in too much pain. I think it was harder for him than for me because my life centered on making his life as comfortable as possible, and I really didn't have time to reflect on what we were missing socially. It's different when you're lying in a hospital or rehab bed and have long stretches of time to think about the life you once had, a life without medical treatments, therapy sessions, walkers, or wheelchairs.

I'd call our friends and family while on my daily walks around the hospital or rehab grounds, and that kept me connected to what was happening within our social circle. Men usually don't talk on the phone with one another as women enjoy doing. Men would rather conduct their conversations in person, but Pete was having less and less of that contact. When his friends visited him in the hospital or rehab facility, there were the usual jokes and male-bonding conversations which he really enjoyed. However, his buddies would eventually leave to return to their normal lives, and he'd have to stay at the facility. I know it bothered Pete even though he never complained.

With Pete gone, accepting social invitations is my way of reconnecting with the social life we knew before Pete became so ill. Without the endless appointments and medical treatments, all-day hospital and rehab visits, I now have time to resume past activities. Of course, my "new normal" is knowing that I'm unable to call Pete on his cell phone or curl up next to him in his hospital or rehab bed to share what I've been doing. To be honest, I still tell him these things even though his physical presence isn't here.

My advice for you is to accept social invitations from those people you feel comfortable with, to attend events you'll find interesting and fun where you'll be able to relax and enjoy yourself.

New adventures are always good, too. My sister-in-law Marcia and I recently traveled from Florida to Arizona to visit our sister-in-law Sue, the widow of Pete's older brother Mike.

Sue's health issues don't permit her to travel any longer, so we went to her. It was a fun, four-day trip, and we were so glad we had gone to see Sue before her health worsened.

When I returned, it wasn't to an empty condo because my cats, Riley and Murphy, were waiting to greet me with scolding meows for leaving them and loving purrs to welcome their "mom" back home where she belonged.

There are many interesting thoughts from women who have been widowed on dealing with social invitations:

"Accept them the first year because otherwise you'll stay home. Drive your own car. After that first year, decide what you want to accept. Don't get to the point of staying home for five or six consecutive days, or you won't want to go out." Joyce B.

"Accept them all. Staying home is the worst. Take your own car when you go somewhere. Then you can leave if you have to. Friends will understand." Kathy H.

"Say yes to most things. I don't go to dinner dances anymore. The dinner part was fine, but when the slow dances begin, you're left alone at the table. Weddings aren't as bad because I can dance with my cousins or other single women. There are so many women who have been widowed. I'm entertaining again. I had a dinner party and a Christmas party." Lila S.

"Accept them. I go out with close friends, including couples. We share my husband's funny stories." Ginny G.

"Go if you feel up to it. If you're feeling terribly weepy, tell the people inviting you that you're not ready and don't want to ruin the party. If you feel you can't stay, tell the hostess you had a good time, but you're leaving. Follow up with a note or phone call thanking them for inviting you. If you don't accept in the beginning, when you're ready, people will have written you off. You might cry all the way home. When the time comes to leave, it hits you that you're going to go home alone. Realize many people are uncomfortable about inviting new widows." Barb W.

"If someone asks you to go to lunch, and you're available, accept. I didn't realize when I discontinued my phone's landline that there would be many of my friends who wouldn't have my cell phone number. I'm not getting as many calls now, but I'm going to start calling people to give them my cell number." Jan B.

"Absolutely accept! What do you have to lose? I like to play bridge and love golf. Be careful of how much money you're spending. I find I'm declining more invitations. I'm very content to finish my social day at 7:00 P.M. when I start to wind down, but I'm still up until 1:00 A.M. at home." Audrey C.

"Pick and choose. Dinners or house parties are okay. Usually, men are on one side and women are on the other. I like to go where there's not dancing. Accept social invitations because you can meet new friends. Treasure time spent with girlfriends." Ruby C.

"I accepted social invitations because new experiences worked for me. I liked being with our close friends because if I had to leave abruptly, they'd understand. For me to always stay home alone would be self-induced sadness, to invite a 'pity party.'" Jolene M.

"Accept because you can make new friends." Joan A.

"After my husband died, close friends from high school who had known him invited me to Florida, and I accepted their invitation. When my husband was working, I used to go places alone. Then, after he died, I didn't do that. I don't get invited to as many places now. If I get invited somewhere, whether or not I accept depends on who it's with and where it is." Lyn L.

"There's been no change for me since my husband died. My advice is to accept those invitations you want and don't feel obligated to go where you don't want to." Carole C.

"If you feel comfortable accepting an invitation, accept it." Gladi B.

"Accept social invitations from friends, or they'll think you're not interested and will forget about you. Try not to bore friends by talking about your loss or your health problems. That will turn them off. Laugh a lot even at things that aren't that funny. Laughing releases healthy endorphins. That first year you'll get a lot of invitations. By the second year, people think, *Oh, she's okay*, and don't invite you as much. When I'm traveling by car and going to be staying at a friend's home for one to two days, I'll take them out to dinner. Something else I do is to take my own sheets, towels, and washcloths. I'll put my own sheets right over theirs, and when I leave, I take my sheets off the bed, and there are their clean sheets. That way they don't have to change their sheets just because someone stayed overnight for one or two nights. The people I stay with are always glad to see me because I leave no 'footprint' that I was there. Another thing, if you expect to be invited places, you have to invite people over. Social invitations are not one-way streets." Lee M.

"At times, it's hard to go, even to a party with my neighbors, but many single women are there, which is nice. Getting out helps. You can't stay home all the time." Mary B.

"Be selective in what you accept. I often feel lonelier in a group than I do by myself. Your couple friends won't be there forever. You're not in the couples' world anymore." Evelyn C.

"Go! If you're not having a good time, leave. If you don't go, you won't know if it's something you would have enjoyed. You might even meet a new friend." Marijo Z.

"I accept all of them." Judie N.

"I usually accepted them. The Rotary Club, which was my husband's hangout, gave me an open invitation to attend meetings. I make sure to tell them the invitation is appreciated. The Rotary Club named a park in my husband's name as a memorial to him. I go to visit the park when my daughter and I go to an art fair nearby." Lou H.

"Pick and choose. Everything falls into place. Decide whom you want to be with. You want to eat with people who don't complain about everything. After a while, you can cut back. You need a few good friends, not acquaintances. Don't judge people. Everyone has their own thing, which might not be right for you." Carol L.

"It depends on who is inviting you. If you really want to go and enjoy their company, go! Go on vacations with friends if you really enjoy it." Nancy J.

"Go! Get together with friends!" Shirley W.

"Accept only if you want. Some people feel obligated to invite you. Most of my friends are single. I play cards two times a month and play dominoes once a month. I belong to two different card clubs. One is made up of all single women and the other is made up of all single women except for one couple." Joanne W.

"I say accept everything. You may have to go alone. Bring a bottle of wine or flowers. Be sure to tell your hosts how much you appreciate being asked and included. You can pick and choose what to accept. Accept the invitations and go! I play bridge twice monthly. Only two who play are single. The rest of the group are married or with partners." Angie O.

"Accept most of them, but you don't always want to be with women." Pearl G.

"Yes! If you're invited, go! You have to step out of your comfort zone. Find a group you're comfortable with. I find myself doing things with single women. When someone asks you to go somewhere, go! The laundry will be waiting for you to do later. Have a short pity party and then get out and do things." Beverly K.

"Should you accept social invitations? Yes! Yes! Yes! Keeping busy is important." Kay P.

"Absolutely accept! Don't be afraid to entertain. It doesn't have to be fancy. I have many single friends. We used to have cocktails at my house, go to lunch, go to another friend's house for dessert. Now we just get together. I decided to go on a cruise a radio talk show host had organized. I had a good time and met a lot of nice people." Barb B.

"If you think you can do it, go. One of the best things for you is being with others. Don't hide like a hermit. If you think it's going to be a downer or a pity party, opt out nicely." Bobbi V.

"Accept them when you feel comfortable. You can go out during the day with friends. It doesn't have to be something major. You can go for a bike ride, shopping, or visit a neighbor." Debbi C.

"After my husband died, I first turned down invitations because I was emotional. I'd cry and didn't want to do it in front of people. Then I began to accept invitations. The best thing is to go. Get out of your comfort zone. Don't do anything unless you want to." Sandy G.

And a final thought:

"I want to stress that after the first year, you have to make an effort to keep friendships and to continue your old social lifestyle. You don't have to accept all social invitations you receive. If you don't want to accept, you can say, 'Maybe we could do something another time.' Or you can just say that you're having a 'bum day' if you don't want to go. You'll settle in as time goes on. I'm getting more used to being alone. If you're feeling down or sorry for yourself, start reading a book or do something else. Have something you like to do when you're home alone. At night, I'd rather go out with other single women." Kay J.

Ask yourself—

After reading the chapter on "Social Invitations," what were my immediate thoughts?

_____

_____

_____

_____

The people I'm most comfortable with are

_____

_____

_____

_____

_____

Which places do I feel most comfortable in besides my home?

_____

_____

_____

_____

_____

What did I find most interesting about the comments made by the women?

_____

_____

_____

_____

_____

What advice would I give a newly- widowed woman about accepting social invitations?

_____

_____

_____

_____

_____

What I want to remember from this chapter:

_____

_____

_____

_____

_____

CHAPTER 20
It's a Couples' World

Staying Connected With Married Friends When You're No Longer a Couple

That it's a couples' world is something you might vaguely be aware of when you're married, but the reality of it doesn't really register until you're suddenly single. Your friends are divided into two groups, those who have husbands or significant others and those who are single. You now fall into the second category, and you'll need to make adjustments. Keep in mind, we're dealing here with your present status, not what may occur in the future.

If you and your husband were socially active, as Pete and I were, you probably socialized with many couples over the years. You've been there for one another through good times and bad, including personal losses. Now you're about to learn who comes through for you when you most need them. Much of their response will depend on the strength of the bonds you've formed with these couples.

For most of the seven years after Pete's MDS diagnosis, we were able to continue our active social life. However, during the last two years of his illness, that began to change as the disease took its toll on Pete's health. That was when I began to email updates to our friends and family telling them what was happening in our lives.

We weren't able to be in Wisconsin as often due to Pete's participation in an MDS clinical trial at Moffitt Cancer Center in Tampa, Florida. Instead of returning to Wisconsin for April through November, we could only return for short two-week stays to check on the house and sporadically see friends and family.

During that last Wisconsin summer filled with hospital and rehab stays, many of our friends would visit and offer support to both of us. Sometimes it would be Pete's buddies, and sometimes it would be couples. When we returned to Florida in November, we had another close-knit group of friends waiting to support us. I mention this because the ties we had with these friends had been strengthened over the course of many years. The email updates I had been sending kept us connected with friends who never felt left out of what Pete and I were experiencing.

Pete passed in May of 2018, and I began writing this book the following November. Our couple friends have been there for me since the beginning of my widowhood. They've continued to include me in the same social events Pete and I participated in with them.

Never forget that continuing these friendships is a two-way street. Just as I wrote in a previous chapter, there's nothing stopping you from doing the inviting or asking if you can ride along to an event. Even close friends sometimes need to be reassured you're still interested in being with them, even if you're not a couple anymore. I've been told by other women that these invitations may lessen as time passes, but, so far, I see no sign of that happening. I can promise you I'm going to do whatever I can to insure the friendships Pete and I shared with these couples continue.

Women who have been widowed have their own ideas on dealing with the "Couples' World."

"Expect to feel uncomfortable in the beginning. You may feel like a fifth wheel. You'll need to force yourself to go because you can't stay home and become a recluse. It will get easier. It's easier if there are five or seven people (including you) when you go out (two or three couples and you). That's because there will be more women, and the men will have other men to talk to. It's more awkward with just one couple because the man doesn't always want to listen to 'girl talk.' When you make reservations at a restaurant, be sure to tell them there will be an odd number like five or seven for dinner. If they seat you at a table for six or eight, it's very uncomfortable seeing that empty chair. Even if they take the extra place setting away, it makes you feel bad. People who are couples are often uncomfortable with you as a single, especially if you're younger. They're not sure what to talk about. It is a couples' society, and you can feel out of place." Barb W.

"I have no problem going out with couples. I have close couple friends who do things with me. I'll go to dinner with two couples and go to lunch with couples. You can invite your couple friends over for dinner. Don't hesitate to do things with couples or to invite them over to your place." Barb B.

"I'm always included. My brother-in-law, who is a widower, always makes sure they include me when other couples are having events, like a Fourth of July party or a Christmas Eve get-together. If it's something I did before, I'm always included. I find myself doing stuff with single women, but I did that before my husband died. These are friends I had when he was alive, like the girls in my card club." Joanne W.

"I still have trouble being with couples after nine years. It's better for me being with single women for dinner. When you go with couples, they don't want you to pay." Mary B.

"There's no question that it's a couples' world. You are no longer a couple. Don't let your feelings get hurt when people don't call you. Two couples didn't call me anymore after my husband died because they didn't want to do things with a widow. They were what I call 'couple friends.' It's really hard to listen to married friends bitch about stupid things regarding their husbands. I say, 'At least you still have him.'" Lee M.

"When I had the store, people would say, 'Oh, I'm going to call you,' but then they didn't. My husband's family saved me. They were constantly there for me and still are." Marijo Z.

"It's a couples' world. I continue to go out with friends, couples who knew my husband and me, and I never feel like a fifth wheel." Jolene M.

"You might feel awkward going out to dinner. It might feel more comfortable going to a friend's home and bringing something. After my husband passed, I was still included with couples, actually more than before, because he had been sick, and we hadn't done much socializing. However, when I went to the theater with two couples, it did feel awkward." Debbi C.

"I still get together with couples my husband and I used to do things with." Joan A.

"I'm so lucky. The couples we used to do things with still include me. I'm still leading my life the way we had. I'm so grateful. Life is more normal. When you go out to dinner with couples, you have to figure out a way to pay for your own meal. Otherwise, when you call them to go out, they'll think they have to pay for you. I'll discreetly ask the waiter to give me a separate bill. If they do pay for your meal, you can repay them by having them over for dinner. When you're out with couples, don't just talk about 'women's' interests. I had two couples over to watch a basketball game, and we had a fun time." Kay J.

"It's very difficult. You don't want to be a burden or have couple friends feel responsible for you. You need to find single female friends. They will understand your feelings. Couples won't understand, and couples aren't supposed to understand. Your situation is not theirs. I like to call myself single, not a widow. I think it's healthier." Evelyn C.

"If you go to dinner with a couple, ask for separate checks. Take your own car. I've found during the first five years after your husband has passed, you're often invited out by couples. You get less invitations to join couples over time. The couples slowly back away. Don't be surprised if this happens." Lila S.

"You need a network of other single women. On Valentine's Day I bought myself flowers. Sometimes when you're with couples, you can feel like a fifth wheel. Some couples stopped calling. These were couples we weren't as close to, more superficial relationships. A friend of mine said she had been by herself having a pity party and decided she wouldn't continue to do that. She put together a list of single women she knew, and they informally meet once a month. If she wants to go to an event and needs someone to go with her, she can call one of the women in the group." Joyce B.

"Yes, I do get together with a lot of friends who have be-come widows. It is definitely a couples' world. I'd like to take a cruise, but it's easier with a spouse. Maybe a widowed friend would go with me." Lyn L.

"Yes, I do get together with couples, but now I do things with just the wives." Carole C.

"I haven't gotten together with couple friends too much. I've been really bad about that. One of the husbands would pick me up at the airport. One time when he was going to pick me up, he said his wife couldn't make it, but he and I would go out to dinner. That made me very uncomfortable, so I asked my brother-in-law to meet us at the restaurant." Sandy G.

"Most couples we used to see still include me. I miss Saturday nights with my husband. I'll go to our club a lot because it's close to home, and I feel comfortable there. Getting invited out by couples is a two-way street. I'll have 'soup parties' but not for more than eight people. I'll make two different kinds of soup, maybe ham and bacon and New England clam chowder, and add homemade rolls. I'll serve only nuts before dinner so my guests don't lose their appetites. I'll serve one soup first, wash out the soup bowls, then serve the other soup. You can also invite a couple or two to dinner." Kay P.

"I find being with couples can be awkward at times since he's passed." Judie N.

"We had one group we were close to, and after he died, they disappeared. They wouldn't return my calls, and I was very hurt that they dropped me after I was widowed. Another couple was close to us and stayed with me before moving to Florida. Because of the time difference, I had to call them in the morning. They didn't understand that widows go through depression and that I wasn't getting up early in the morning." Lou H.

"I still get together with couples my husband and I used to do things with." Joan A.

"The couples we did things with are no longer couples because spouses have died. I have a few very dear friends. I moved on to find my own group of friends, had to find my own space where I was comfortable. If you're friends with the wife, the husband may not be comfortable with you. You're her friend, not his. You need to figure it out. You could meet the wife for lunch rather than meet both of them for dinner." Carol L.

"I didn't give up on couples; they gave up on me. Many couples are apprehensive of you being around." Pearl G.

"Many times when you lose a spouse, the couples just ignore you. I don't see much of the couples we did things with. Some even called me and said they felt 'funny' calling and inviting me because it didn't feel right without my husband. I went out with one of my girlfriends. I also went out to a neighborhood bar where my husband and I played darts. People were so nice and made me feel so welcome. They even invited me to parties. I don't drink anymore because of the meds I'm taking." Nancy J.

"I'm in my eighties, so there aren't many couples left in my group of friends." Shirley W.

"I think the world has changed somewhat. I don't think it's a couples' world anymore. There are more women in business who travel and sightsee alone. Younger women aren't getting married like they used to. The gay movement helped single people. Insurance companies now cover gay partners. I traveled with a group of women. Even women who are married want to get out with other women. I felt safe with married couples. I had that and liked it. Now I've remarried." Kathy H.

"Couples in Wisconsin stopped calling me. It's okay to be single in The Villages, where I live in Florida. It's very normal and very comfortable to live there. To see if I would like living in The Villages, I rented a vacation home there and thought to myself, *I can function here*. The only group in Wisconsin that included me was the bridge group." Angie O.

"In the future you might meet someone through your friends who are couples. I was always included and didn't feel like a fifth wheel." Debbi C.

"I never had an issue going out with our friends who are couples." Ginny G.

"I think it's harder if you're younger because a lot of wives think you might flirt with their husbands." Ruby C.

"I don't hear from many of the couples we used to see. It suddenly hit me that's because I took the landline out, and not everyone has my cell phone number. I am going to lunch with some of the couples." Jan B.

"It certainly is a couples' world. It's not like it was before with the couples we knew; now one spouse is gone from many of the couples." Audrey C.

And a final thought:

"It is a couples' world. You have to work at staying close to former couple friends to make the friendships last. For me, I think it's more awkward to go out with just one couple because you have to give attention to both the husband and the wife. If you're out with two or more couples, it's easier to spread the conversation among the group." Beverly K.

Ask yourself—

What are my immediate thoughts after reading the chapter "The Couples' World"?

_____

_____

_____

_____

Here are some ways for me to stay connected with my friends who are couples:

_____

_____

_____

_____

_____

The advice I would give a newly widowed woman with regard to staying in touch with the couples she and her husband socialized with would be:

_____
_____
_____
_____
_____

What I want to remember after reading this chapter:

_____
_____
_____
_____
_____

CHAPTER 21
Dating

"I Have Someone I Want You to Meet" Oh—Oh!

Exactly one week and one day after Pete's Wisconsin funeral, my friends and I were leaving a club function when an elderly member stopped me and asked how I was doing. Mind you, this gentleman had attended Pete's funeral and had known us for many years. I replied I was doing fine and thanked him for asking. The rest of the brief conversation went as follows:

Him—"That's good. I have a man I want you to meet."

Me—"Thanks, but I'm really not interested."

Him—"You'd like him. He just lost his wife." (Now, that's definitely a referral a recent widow doesn't want to hear.)

Me—"I'm really not interested."

Him—"It would just be dinner."

Me—"I'm not interested, and I'm leaving. Bye."

My girlfriends standing behind him heard this exchange, rolled their eyes, and couldn't believe what they were hearing. Later, the girls and I had a good laugh, and I did take the gentleman's age into consideration in excusing his insensitivity. Let's face it: I'm sure he meant well.

Pete always told me that if anything ever happened to him, he wouldn't want me to be alone, and that I'd have to "fight the guys off with a stick." That was my husband's high opinion of me. Believe me, after losing the best husband I could ever have had, dating is the last thing on my mind.

A single friend of mine told me I had no idea what I was about to experience with people trying to "fix me up" now that I was a widow. Another of my widowed friends repeated a phrase she had heard in a bereavement group: "Women grieve and men replace."

Think about it; that is so true. When I was making funeral arrangements, the funeral director told me, "Bonnie, you're going to do just fine. Women handle losing a spouse much better than men do. Men don't handle losing a spouse well at all." That made me think about my widowed friends and how the majority of them have not rushed to fill the void left by a husband's passing. On the other hand, many of the widowers I know have not hesitated to jump into the dating pool a relatively short time after losing their wives. I'm guessing it's probably due to loneliness and subconsciously needing someone to take care of the everyday things in much the same way their wives did. I also believe husbands share more personal things with their wives than they do with other men, and widowers miss not being able to do that.

Another piece of cautionary advice from a friend is that when men get older, many are looking for a "nurse or a purse." This phrase was restated by another friend to "older men are looking for nurses WITH purses." It may sound somewhat humorous, but there's a grain of truth to that statement.

There's a difference between being alone and being lonely. As social as I am, I've never been a person who is uncomfortable being alone. There are my cats, Riley and Murphy, and friends and family to keep me company. My time is filled with activities that interest me, and writing this book has certainly occupied much of my time.

Am I saying I'll never go on a date in the future? No, I'm not. What I am saying is that right now dating is definitely not on my list of priorities. My dear eighty-nine-year-old friend Gladi has been widowed twice and tells me that she hopes that when the time is right, I'll find someone, not necessarily to marry but to share things with. I consider that to be wise advice from a very wise woman.

During their interviews, women who had been widowed had very strong opinions on dating and some very valuable advice.

"Tread slowly when going out on dates. Drive your own car. Go to a place where there are lots of people. Never go to a hotel room or apartment on a first date or even early on in dating. Find out if the man is married. You don't have to ask right away but let it come up in the conversation. A man I had a first (and only) dinner date with said to me when I asked if he was married, 'Well, I am married, but we're having problems.' I told him, 'Your problems aren't my problems,' and never went out with him again. When I was working, I started getting flowers at home with no name on them. Because the sender knew where I lived, I brought it to the attention of the HR person at my place of work. It turned out to be a customer thanking me for helping him, but I felt safer telling someone. I was seventy when I married my second husband after twenty-eight years as a widow. It's nice to have someone to talk with, to go to the movies with. Women are nice company, but it's nice, too, to have a man to share things with. Keep things open." Gladi B.

"After eight years, I'm open to the possibility but not seeking dates. I went on a date after two years of being widowed and didn't enjoy it. Make up your mind as to what it is you want. Do you want dinner now and then, or do you want a long-term relationship? I'm a golfer and went online to the Golfmates dating website. I met someone, and he now golfs with our golf group up north." Lila S.

"It's an individual choice. You'll know if and when you're ready. Take baby steps. Some people need to be part of a couple. That's not dishonoring the memory of your past life.

You can't be locked into thinking there's a certain amount of time you need to wait before dating or that you're never going to date again. Be careful and play it safe. Meet in a public place during the daytime. Be prepared for meeting both great guys and creeps. You have to see the humor in situations. You have to think like a strong woman. Ask yourself, *Will this relationship benefit me?* Never let them see you sweat. The scales need to be balanced. If the relationship seems to be one-sided, you can leave because you're not married. If someone becomes a stalker, call the police. After eight or nine months after my husband passed, I wanted to go out with someone of the opposite sex." Bobbi V.

"I have no interest in dating. I haven't met anyone I'd want to date or marry." Barb B.

"I was forty-two when I was widowed. Maybe one year went by before I went on some blind dates, which felt awkward. You might enjoy it more if you meet a blind date when you're with a group of friends. Friends of mine brought their cousin to a Christmas party at my home. It was a relaxed setting, we clicked, and now we're married!" Debbi C.

"It's scary. There are lunatics out there. Even if a date has been referred to you by a friend, be cautious. With online dating, anyone can put together any kind of profile. Men on dating sites are often looking for younger women. If I hadn't previously known my partner, who was a friend of my husband, I wouldn't have dated." Barb W.

"Not interested." Beverly K.

"I met a friend of a friend, and we went to a movie and dinner. It was companionship. All of a sudden, he was gone. I see him when other people are around but wouldn't date him again. If you want to see someone, you could say, 'A bunch of us are going to lunch (or breakfast). Do you want to join us?' I wouldn't remarry." Kay P.

"I'm open to it but haven't even had a cup of coffee with someone. I've closed my mind to remarriage. I have no need to go online to a dating website. I think about men my age wanting a 'nurse with a purse.'" Pearl G.

"Four years after my husband died, my bridge group invited me to play with a partner who had lost his wife and had two young children. He had no idea that I was ten years older than he was. I went out with him once to see if I could handle it. Once was enough. I still played cards with him. I don't have to worry about dating because I don't need anything more than what I have." Angie O.

"No one has tried to fix me up. I miss holding hands, something my husband and I always did. I miss the intimacy of going out to a nice dinner with someone. It's also a vanity issue when it comes to dating. I don't physically look like I did in my thirties. My husband knew how I looked when I was that age. I wouldn't remarry." Joanne W.

"No one ever tried to fix me up." Shirley W.

"I don't care about dating. Why should I? My son in Kansas City wanted me to meet a retired engineer. I said, 'Why should I?' Four years ago I was shopping, and a guy at a grocery store sample counter gave me his business card. Why should I call him? I'm not interested." Ginny G.

"No dating. A classmate called two years ago and wanted to take me to dinner. I thought we'd be with a group, but it was just the two of us. After that, he called every day and wanted to talk for two hours. I was doing taxes and didn't have time to talk. He wouldn't get off the phone. Finally, I told him I wasn't interested and wouldn't stay on the phone. I told him I didn't want to take care of another sick person." Nancy J.

"I'm grateful no one has asked me, but I'm eighty-seven, so that's not an option. I wouldn't consider dating, but if an old friend called, I'd go to dinner with him. I prefer being with couples. My opinion is that men want to date women because men don't talk to other men like women talk to girlfriends. Men want to talk to a woman." Kay J.

"Absolutely not! I've been asked out, but I'm not interested. Many men are looking for a caretaker. Men are helpless without wives. I'm content with what I had." Carol L.

"Some guys are set in their ways and don't even 'see' you. Guys have what I call a 'man shield.' My husband lowered his when he became ill. That's when our relationship became even closer." Lou H.

"It's too soon for me to even think about dating. It's only been eleven months since he passed, not even a year." Judie N.

"It's been seven years, and no one has tried to fix me up. I've not really dated. Once I went to dinner with a younger man and was very uncomfortable. I've not gotten into the dating scene. I'd love to have someone to do fun stuff with. I miss the touching, hugging, and holding hands that is part of a relationship. It's sad not to have someone to share things with. I'll tell you one thing, if you do date a guy with children, do not mess with his kids. That means keep your mouth shut if his kids are bratty. He'll always side with his kids." Lee M.

"One year after my husband died, my brother-in-law wanted me to meet his best friend. I met him, and he became my second husband. He died ten months later." Marijo Z.

"If someone asks you if you're dating, why should it matter to them? It's not their business. I haven't been able to bridge to dating life. There's no timeline as to when you should date. When you do date, know who that person is seated across from you. Know his history. Have mutual friends. I don't recommend online dating. If you remarry, remember that everything you bring into the marriage with your new husband now becomes community property and his heirs have a right to it unless you have a prenuptial agreement." Evelyn C.

"Oh, no! I have no interest in dating! I'm not going to 'train' another husband! I don't even want to go out social-ly for dinner. One of my friends went out with a man and thought it was strictly social. The man became controlling, tried to cut her off from her friends, and said he wanted a wife. She won't see him again." Mary B.

"My husband died in September. The following June, I met our doctor for coffee, and we talked for hours. His wife had died, and I had known her because our daughters had started school together. He and I knew we weren't getting married. It was about companionship, traveling together. We were together for eight years before he died from a stroke." Lyn L.

"It's too soon to think of dating. It's only been nine months." Joan A.

"A month after my husband died, a guy at work began hitting on me. I did the 'widow's run' (Chapter 22) and got away from him. One of my girlfriends would do a background check on any guy paying attention to me." Jolene M.

"Never say never, but I'm not interested. I know a couple of women who have met men online and are happy. They're not going to get married but are living together." Ruby C.

"That (dating) remains to be seen. The widowed husband of a friend invited me out on New Year's Eve. That was sweet of him, but I couldn't go because I was in Florida." Audrey C.

"It's too soon for me." Sandy G.

"I'm not interested, but it would be nice to eat with someone; then I wouldn't have to be by myself. They wouldn't have to buy my dinner. My second husband worked with my first husband. His wife died the same year as my husband. He asked me to dinner. I wanted to help him get through his wife's death. I was not chasing him. He called me twenty times a day. He was older than my first husband, but they were very similar. If I hadn't known him before, I wouldn't have dated." Jan B.

"A woman doctor told me, 'You'll never find anyone like your husband, but if you find someone you'd like to date, I want you to remember three things: one, use protection to prevent an STD (sexually transmitted disease); two, be careful of predators; and three, be careful of your heart.' I don't have a desire to date, but I miss hanging out with guys. If there's some guy you like and want to see, go for it. There's no right or wrong. Six weeks after my husband died, friends came over for dinner. The husband said he had a colleague he wanted me to meet. His wife punched him in the arm and said, 'I can't believe you just said that!'" Joyce B.

And a final thought:

"Widows are so vulnerable. You think everyone can be trusted like you trusted your husband, but it's a different world, not the world we knew. You can be smart with finances, etc., but when it comes to love, you can be very vulnerable. You never have to settle. If the relationship is easy and flows, then it's right. If you have to worry about what he's doing when you're not with him, then it's wrong. Be careful. You were in a trustful relationship, and there are guys out there who can't be trusted. Take it slowly. You're very vulnerable. You believe guys because you had a trustful relationship with your husband. Be direct and honest with guys. No game playing." Kathy H.

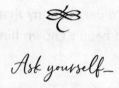

Ask yourself—

What are my immediate thoughts after reading this chapter on "Dating"?

_____

_____

_____

_____

_____

The comments I found most interesting were:

_____

_____

_____

_____

The advice I would give someone who was recently widowed if she asked about dating is:

_____

_____

_____

_____

What I want to remember from this chapter:

_____

_____

_____

_____

_____

CHAPTER 22
The "Widow's Run"

"I've Got to Get Out of Here—NOW!"

You may not be familiar with the term "widow's run." I wasn't until one of the women being interviewed asked if I had ever experienced it. I asked her what the term meant, and she explained, "That's when you're out somewhere, and all of a sudden you tell yourself you have to leave...immediately!" There doesn't have to be a specific reason for your speedy exit; it's more of a feeling that you can't remain there any longer without risking your emotional health.

My widow's run came shortly after I learned what it meant. I was at a club meeting, after a year's absence, and everyone warmly greeted me, expressed condolences for my loss, and were just as nice as they could be. There were too few servers at the restaurant, and our large group waited an extremely long time for our orders. As our wait stretched on, I suddenly realized that I couldn't remain at the restaurant. When our dinner orders arrived, I asked for a carry-out container and the check, said my goodbyes, and left. That was my widow's run. At the next meeting the following month, I was perfectly fine.

Since then I've learned that many women who have been widowed experience this, so know you're not alone if it happens to you.

"Six months after my husband died, there were times when I had to leave church because I knew I was going to get emotional with more than just tears. Six weeks after he died, I went to a wedding where I didn't know a lot of people. I was fine, visited with my table mates, and made it through the dinner. Then the music began. At the second song, I got up and knew I had to leave." Beverly K.

"I have it often, sometimes at house parties. At dinner dances when the music begins, I'm out of there." Lila S.

"At home, I started rereading the sympathy cards and started to cry. After that, if I wanted to reread them, I'd do it later at night, so I could 'run' to bed if I felt bad." Kay P.

"Have an escape plan. Always have something worked out in your head, 'This is what I'm going to say,' so you don't fumble around when you're saying your goodbyes. If you feel you have to go, tell your hostess or ask someone to tell her you had to leave. Follow up the next day with a phone call. If you're in a restaurant, try to get through the meal. Follow up the next day with something like 'I'm sure you understand. It's nothing you did.'" Barb W.

"I was in a grocery store and suddenly I got the feeling of being closed in, like there were too many people. I said to myself, *I'm outta here*, put my shopping cart back, and left the store. However, I didn't have a problem after that when I went to an art fair or other places where there were a lot people." Angie O.

"I went to my fiftieth high school reunion and felt like I had to leave. I've been at a party, sneaked out, and went home. I don't think anyone even knew I had left. If you know the people well, it's okay." Barb B.

"My widow's run was at my husband's memorial service. There were too many people offering condolences. I felt supported, but there were too many tears." Bobbi V.

"I went to a cocktail party that I had already paid for at my club. I got to the door and found I couldn't make myself go inside. I just left." Lee M.

"I went to a party that went from 8:00 to 11:00. I could only stay an hour. You'll develop different habits. It's easier now because when you're older, you get fewer invitations. People are dying, and life goes on." Pearl G.

"If I realized an event wouldn't be good for me, I simply didn't go. If I did go and felt claustrophobic or felt myself begin to panic, I would leave and ask a close friend there to explain." Jolene M.

"I was at a wedding, and they started showing family pictures on a screen. I had to leave. Another time, a friend had a party at his house, and another person brought pictures of a trip she, her husband, and their family had taken. I had to leave because that family part of my life was gone." Kathy H.

"Yes, I've had that. I was somewhere with friends, and all of a sudden, I felt like I was being choked or smothered, and it was like I was having a panic attack. I asked my friends to take me home. It wasn't far." Nancy J.

"I don't have it too much because I try not to put myself in those situations. Once I was at a Super Bowl party and felt like it was time to leave at half-time." Kay J.

"I've not really experienced it. I've put my guard up and established lines about where I want to be. I think people who can't make decisions about where they want to be have more problems." Carol L.

"I was in church when a wave of grief hit me. I started crying, but I thought, *I can't just leave*, so I stayed. But I wanted to run." Lou H.

"I was out with a couple the night before I was leaving to go back home. They were drinking, and I was at the end of my rope. After dinner, I said I had to leave because I had things to do." Marijo Z.

"Yes, I've experienced it if something brought back memories or feelings." Gladi B

"I guess you could call this a widow's run. I'll get invitations on Facebook from men I don't know wanting me to 'friend' them. I never do." Joan A.

"It's not really a widow's run, but a friend is 180 degrees from my political views, and I told her we are NOT discussing politics! Now I just don't feel like listening and want to run when she starts." Audrey C.

"Yes, I had that mostly after my first husband died. A good friend wanted me to come over. I went, but I couldn't stay there." Jan B.

"Dinner dances are a no-no. When the dancing begins, you're left alone at the table. The last dinner dance I went to, I got short of breath and had to leave." Evelyn C.

And a final thought:

"The first Father's Day without my husband was eight months after he died. I was at the kids' house, and they were talking about how if they asked one group out to the lake, they'd have to ask another, and the circle kept increasing. I was at the sink, and hearing the discussion got to be too much for me. I left and went for a long walk. Remember, you have limited energy, you're still vulnerable, and your heart is still tender." Joyce B.

The "Widow's Run"

Ask yourself—

What are my immediate thoughts after reading the chapter "The 'Widow's Run'" ?

_____

_____

_____

_____

_____

Do I think I've ever experienced this and, if I have, when did it occur?

_____

_____

_____

_____

_____

Even though it may happen when I least expect it, what precautions could I take to help guard against it?

_____

_____

_____

_____

_____

What do I want to remember from this chapter?

_____

_____

_____

_____

_____

CHAPTER 23
Playing the "Widow's Card"
Use Sparingly & Only When Absolutely Necessary!

O f course you don't want people feeling sorry for you after your loss, but sometimes you'll find that it doesn't
hurt to let someone know you've recently lost your husband
when you need a little extra "ammunition" to get something
done or to get a point across.

Our storage shed in the back of the property was badly
damaged when two huge trees fell onto it. My cousin Marilyn
and I salvaged what we could and then stacked the rest in
the driveway, taking up half its fifty-foot length. The garbage pickup was due in two days, and I called the sanitation
company to see what was acceptable for collection. Along
with the smaller miscellaneous items, I had larger items
like a leaf collector, broken wheelbarrow, seed thrower, a
hand lawnmower that had seen better days, leaky hoses,
and long pieces of metal from the shed's roof. The woman
who answered said the larger items could only be taken one
per week, the shingles from the shed had to be stacked into
twelve-inch piles and tied with twine, and numerous items I

mentioned weren't eligible to be picked up at all.

I had no idea what to do with the non-eligible items, but I did take each of the larger items to my neighbors' driveways to be picked up with their garbage. It was ninety degrees outside as I began stacking and tying up the shingles until I ran out of twine. Suddenly, the garbage men arrived. I told them my husband had recently passed, the shed had collapsed when the trees fell on it, and I needed to get rid of what was in the driveway. I asked what they could take, and, bless their hearts, they took all of it! The next week they found a large bag of chocolate chip cookies waiting for them.

As stated in this chapter's subtitle, you don't want to play the "widow's card" often, but it doesn't hurt to keep it in reserve for select situations.

From the following stories told by women who have been widowed, you'll see that I'm not the only independent woman who has played this card effectively.

"I tried it with the garbage men, but it didn't work. My car died. I went to my neighbors across the street and said to the man who lived there, 'I'm sorry, but I'm alone and need help.' His wife was upset with me for asking. He came over, looked at the car, and told me where to go to get it fixed. After that episode, I called AAA when I need help with the car." Angie O.

"Sometimes you need to play it over dumb stuff. I've used it with the garbage men. I got mad at the car dealership when the girl I was talking to on the phone couldn't give me an answer to my question. When I asked for the manager, he told me when the phones get overloaded, calls are transferred to an answering service. I said, 'As a widow I come here because I trust you.' My oil change was free of charge." Pearl G.

"After my husband died, I missed a house payment, and the banker called about it. I told him my husband had just died and started to cry. The banker said it would be okay. When I'm asked for donations to some group, I'll say, 'My finances have changed.'" Joyce B.

"I went to dinner with a widow who had the same wedding anniversary as we did. I had made reservations. We waited one hour, and when I asked how much longer we'd have to wait, the hostess said they didn't take reservations for two people. I told her no one had told me that, that it was Christmas, that we were both widows who had the same anniversary. We were seated. Another time, I rented a place on vacation, and the owner didn't want to return my security deposit even though I hadn't caused any damage. After I protested, he said he'd give half of the deposit back to me. I said no. I read him the Bible verse that said not to take advantage of a widow or God will smite your children. He said, 'Are you threatening my children?' I said, 'Just think of that the next time you take communion.' (I knew he was Catholic.) I had the complete security deposit back soon after." Beverly K.

271

"Use it if you're in a situation where the problem needs to be resolved. It's another weapon in your arsenal. Use it sparingly because you don't want to be addicted to pity." Bobbi V.

"The closest I've come to using it was when I sent a letter to a friend asking him to help me disperse my husband's ashes." Debbi C.

"The water softener bags of salt are very heavy. I'm getting it delivered now, and they carry it to the basement for me." Barb B.

"The garbage men know I'm a widow and take everything I put out." Kay P.

"My faucet was leaking, and I asked a friend, 'Should I call a plumber?' He fixed it. Sometimes you don't want to come right out and ask someone to fix something." Lila S.

"I used it on a male teacher when my son was having problems in high school after his dad died. I said that due to the circumstances, my son was having a bad year. The teacher wrote on my son's report that due to the turmoil of the past year, he was passing him." Joanne W.

"I never used it because I was young when I was widowed and didn't want anyone to know I was alone." Kathy H.

"I needed help with the pool. I told the pool tech I had become a widow and never before needed to be the one taking care of it. I asked him what I needed to do. Another time, I didn't know how to stain windows. I went to the

True Value hardware store and asked someone, 'How do I do this? It's the first time I need to do this.' Then I also went to YouTube and learned how to do it myself." Ginny G.

"It wasn't exactly playing the widow's card, but I asked a friend to go with me to the doctor because I didn't want to go alone." Nancy J.

"I will tell people that I'm a widow. I'm clarifying that I'm not a divorcée and that I'm available." Lee M.

"Someone came to repair the furnace, and I asked if he would help me move something. It took just a few minutes, but I couldn't have moved it alone. It was a two-person job." Kay J.

"Number one is always to protect yourself. Have reputable, licensed people in your home. I had someone in my condo to do something, and he asked to use the bathroom. I said no and reported him. He could have gone to McDonald's. He could have looked in my medicine cabinet for drugs. I told his company, 'I'm a single woman in the house.' Don't hesitate to protect yourself, and put your safety first." Carol L.

"I was learning to care for the yard with fertilizer, etc., and needed to know how to do it. I went to Home Depot and told them I was a widow, and they told me how to do it. Ace Hardware is also a good place to ask for help." Lou H.

"Use it if you need help. I needed to buy a different car. I told the owner of the dealership this was the first time I was buying a car and that it was a big decision for me. He sat with me for two hours, and I got a good deal." Evelyn C.

"Oh, sure, I've used it in haggling with AT&T over the bill. I'll say, 'I'm a widow on a fixed income.' You have to fight for what you want." Lyn L.

"My TV wouldn't work, and I called the cable provider. I said, 'I'm alone, there's no sound in this place. I'm alone with no one to talk to.' They still made me wait for a tech." Karen C.

"Absolutely, I've used it. I've asked people to move a TV or heavy furniture. I called a handyman in Florida, and when he arrived, he asked me questions like, 'Are you alone? Don't you have a brother to help you?' I wasn't sure where he was going with those questions and told him my husband had passed, and this was all very new for me. He said, 'I want you to think of me as a brother.' That taught me that people may have different approaches, but they mean well." Jolene M.

"I'm too independent to play the widow's card." Ruby C.

"I'll sometimes ask the guy across the street to help me with something." Jan B.

And a final thought:

"I played the widow's card only once. Actually, I didn't play it; it was dealt to me. My husband died in Florida while our condo was under construction. The workers at the next building were there and saw the ambulance arrive. When I came back to check on the condo and began buying things for it, the workers knew he had died and would come over to help me empty the car. They said they were sorry for me. They helped carry in groceries. The foreman said they would fix anything in my condo first. They were so concerned for me." Barb W.

Ask yourself—

What are my immediate thoughts after reading the chapter "Playing the 'Widow's Card'" ?

_____

_____

_____

_____

_____

Do I feel an independent woman can play that card and still remain independent?

_____

_____

_____

_____

_____

What advice could I give someone about playing the widow's card when she feels it's necessary?

_____

_____

_____

_____

_____

What do I want to remember from this chapter?

_____

_____

_____

_____

CHAPTER 24
Filling Your Time

There's a Big World Out There

If you're working, your job or career is going to fill much of your time. However, working or not, those hours that you and your husband spent together are still going to be there. You needn't feel you have to frantically fill every moment of the day, especially at the beginning of your widowhood. Take time to heal and consider options. I call it "lying low in the weeds and licking your wounds." Much of the time early on is filled with everything that needs to be done after a husband passes, all the cancelations, switching things over to your name, notifications, perhaps going through his clothes and deciding what you want to give away to family or friends, donate, or keep.

Once you've completed these immediate tasks, it's time for you—to read, watch TV, crochet, write in a journal, whatever it is that gives you relaxation. You'll know when you feel up to getting out of the house and resuming activities, but don't take too much time before returning to the outside world. Developing a habit of isolation is definitely not healthy for you.

If you want to return to work, then that's an option, If not, there are many places or organizations where you can volunteer your services. Others really do need all the gifts you have to offer. Sunday newspapers usually have a section that lists where volunteers are needed, or you can go online and search volunteer groups in your area.

For nine and a half years, with the exception of the leave I took when Pete was so ill, I've volunteered once a week at AngelsGrace Hospice in Wisconsin, truly a blessed, caring place. We volunteers, who have undergone extensive training, work the front desk greeting visitors, give tours of the facility, take food trays to and from rooms, help feed the patients, answer call lights to see if it's something as simple as a patient wanting a glass of water or needing something from the other side of the room. We sit with patients, make sure there are fresh flowers in the vases, take patients outside when the weather permits, help with office work, and offer support to family members. If we don't feel comfortable doing a task, we aren't required to do it. It's so rewarding for me to volunteer there.

If hospice work is not something you feel comfortable doing, then there are neonatal units at hospitals where newborns are waiting to be held, animal shelters where pets need to be socialized, play groups where schoolchildren are introduced to live theater. Remember to get together with friends and family; they want your company, too. Daily exercise is healthy and benefits you both physically and mentally.

In this chapter, you'll find plenty of suggestions from women who have been widowed for filling your free time.

"I couldn't do a lot at first. It was hard to focus on watching TV or reading books, which I had always enjoyed. Then I felt more joyful as time passed, and I began reading again. I have a great support system of family and friends. I try new experiences like eating at new restaurants or going to concerts in the park. When I don't know what else to do, my go-to routine is to take a bath. It relaxes me and fills an hour. I'm also still working at a job I enjoy and can work from home a lot of the time." Jolene M.

"Get involved. Push yourself to go places. Get brochures from a local senior citizen center to see what they offer. Senior citizen centers offer numerous classes, and many single women are there. Get a single friend to go with you or go by yourself. Call a friend and go to the movies on 'budget day' once or twice a month. Play cards. For three years I chose to volunteer at a hospital in the medical library. While there, I heard so many stories that I said to myself, 'I'm not as bad off as I thought.' There was a little chapel, which was peaceful, near the library." Mary B.

"Make sure you have something to do every day so you have something to look forward to. Join something. When you do things, you get it back tenfold. You want to be able to say to yourself, 'Today I have this to do.' Churches have tons of opportunities for filling your time. I was a hospice volunteer. Reach out to others. Help out at a children's hospital. If you see someone in uniform, thank them for their service. If you can afford it, give them some money and say, 'Have a lunch on me.'" Kathy H.

"I started my 'Chapter Two' group for widows to do things together. I attend the Rep Theater. I work with children in public schools whose parents don't speak English and help them with reading. I'll travel and get together with friends." Ruby C.

"In the beginning, fill your time and keep busy. Then become more selective in what you jump into. You have to get yourself out there. If there's something you always wanted to do, do it. Do whatever your passion is. I've become more involved in my church. Get together with friends, or travel with friends if you're able. You can join a book club or a garden club. I play golf and enjoy card games." Beverly K.

"Make a list of what you like to do. Also make a list of what you'd like to do that you haven't done in years. You can take fun, free classes like arts and crafts. If you like to go to the theater, you could volunteer to usher two or three times a month and get to see the plays. If there's a waiting list for ushers, put your name on it, and do other things until your name comes up. If you like to bike, you could join a bike club. There are many places where you could volunteer. Many health insurance policies belong to the Silver Sneakers program. That gives you free access to many health clubs. If you like to garden, you could join a garden club or go someplace to get ideas. You can take a photography class, and you don't need an expensive camera to do that. Churches offer many activities. You can take online classes. There are so many things you can do." Debbi C.

"Do not sit and mope. Initially, you'll be getting your house in order. Find things that get you involved. Try to be with people. There are card clubs, plays, movie matinees. Churches have so many events. You'll meet others who are single and who want to go out and do things." Barb B.

"Push your boundaries, or continue the interests that you and your husband had. Now you can do what you like to do but he didn't. Take advantage of bus trips. They are offered through churches or banks. There are usually many singles, and you'll meet people. Don't be afraid to go by yourself. There are various interesting groups at churches. Look in the paper for groups. It's the beginning of a different or new normal for you, so incorporate what your husband didn't want to do. I'm a big volunteer advocate. It will put things in perspective for you. I volunteered at a women's help center where we helped women going from prison or welfare to work. I said to myself, 'I might have lost a husband, but these women have nothing.'" Barb W.

"Bite the bullet and show up by yourself. I joined a mixed golf group up north and met a whole new group of people. I learned how to play mahjong. I had to focus on cleaning out my house, and that took a lot of time. I travel with girl-friends or get together with friends." Lila S.

"I sew, knit, and read. There are free lectures to attend. You can go to libraries to find a schedule or go online. Most single people will talk to you but not couples. At the art museum, everyone talks to you. You can take classes on different subjects there. I like to travel. If it's a place within the state, I'll go alone. I'll often go on bus trips with groups. I'll watch TV to fill the time. My mother-in-law always said that I love my sports. I enjoy watching sports and will eat before the game. It adds structure to my time." Pearl G.

"At the end of some days, I'll think, *What did I do? Nothing.* Other days I'll do lots. I'll go through cabinets and drawers and clean them. You can get together with friends for lunch or plays." Lyn L.

"Put yourself out there. You won't get included if you don't ask. I live in The Villages in Florida, and there are so many groups and things to do there. I play bridge. I have my dog-sitting business. I belong to Girls for God, and we meet two times a month. We say prayers and use the book *Rediscover Jesus* by Matthew Kelly as a basis for our group. The Villages has its own newspaper that lists who's speaking. A bus takes us to hear political speakers. You may not agree with all the speakers, but you respect them, and hearing them keeps your mind active. I joined the Wisconsin Club and the Italian Club. There are many day trips; for example, we went to high tea at Disney World. You're not a 'senior' in The Villages; you're just another person going out and doing things. That's why there are so many people in The Villages. There are lists of volunteer opportunities. Retired teachers can read to children at different recreation centers. There are workers in The Villages who live here and have children who go to schools here. The schools in The Villages rank in Florida's top five." Angie O.

"I'm never lonely. I miss my husband, but I'm alone, not lonely. Every church has a lot going on. There are Bible studies, senior groups, and groups that go to soup kitchens to serve food to needy people. You can meet new people through church groups. I don't have to be doing something all the time. I like to have my own time. I'll exercise and walk. It's good to meet with friends and share things." Ginny G.

"I'm not personally big on volunteering, but you can if you like to do that. I spend my time with friends—card clubs, lunch, dinner, Friday senior-priced movies. I'm a blood donor. I love to read. There are a lot of things on my calendar, but I'm happy to come home. I don't have to check in with anyone now. It's all about me. I can do what I want to do. If I want to, I can work out, get together with the girls I used to work with. I like to travel with my brothers and my sister-in-law. Find something that makes you happy and do it. I like that I can do things on the spur of the moment. Definitely, don't put off doing something with friends because you were going to do something at home." Joanne W.

"Stay busy doing things that enrich you. If it doesn't feel right, don't do it. Find a balance between what feels right for you and what's available. In the beginning, I probably jumped into too many things too soon. Now I'm more selective as to what I join. Volunteering is good because you feel like you're helping others. There are a lot of activities through our church, and I traveled with the church group, but not to places my husband and I had gone. I drove to Florida with my granddaughters, and we had so much fun. They're coming down for spring break." Joyce B.

"Do whatever you feel like doing. I read, watch TV, do stuff around the house, go to lunch. Time passes quickly." Shirley W.

"I'm finding more widows who are alone to do things with. I know a widow in the neighborhood who has 'crawled into a hole' and will only go outside of her house to walk her dog. When I try to talk to her, she won't respond and just walks away from me. So sad. I work two days a week doing office work for my friend. There are therapy sessions for me to attend since I had my aortic valve replaced. I'm involved with the Young Timers group through the Boy Scouts. We do a lot of things, including helping the Feeding America association by sorting food in bins for them. There are lots of committees to join at church. We pick names from a tree for Christmas gifts, plan a party for kids, make knit hats. We help with the church cookie sale and rummage sale." Nancy J.

"Get out of the house, volunteer, golf, go to lunch. When you're home alone, do something you enjoy. Try to plan something to look forward to." Kay J.

"I'll go to Target and use my cane to get to the cart rack. Then I'll use one of their carts to lean on and go up and down the aisles. It's safer than walking on the streets, and people are there. Church groups are good. Help someone else. Volunteer for something. You don't have to tie your-self down by committing to so many hours per week. You can fill in for someone. There are people everywhere who need help. You can find volunteer groups in the paper, on-line, or in the phone book. I worked in the soup kitchen. Volunteering is the best cure there is for feeling down. I'll dog-sit for friends. Go to lunch with friends or ask friends to go out to dinner. (P.F. Chang's has gluten-free Chinese food.)" Carol L.

"I'm in two plus bridge clubs and one sheepshead club. At our church, I help a group make greeting cards. I'm a member of our club's auxiliary. I travel and do things with friends." Kay P.

"I've never been bored in my eighty-nine years. There's not enough time to do everything. There are church and volunteer groups. I love to read, but I don't have time right now. I'm trying to get things organized because I have pul-monary fibrosis and don't want my husband's or my papers, etc., left in a mess for our children. Since God has given me extra time, I'm using it the best way I can by participating in genetic familial research studies on pulmonary fibrosis at the University of Colorado and the Mayo Clinic; my seven brothers died of the disease." Gladi B.

"I do a lot of genealogy research on the computer. My daughter and I go 'graveyard looking' and found my great-grandmother's grave. I attend our church's widows/widow-ers group once a month. I'll go to the Rotary Club, where my husband was active, once in a while. I'm fighting fatigue with my health, so I'm sort of limited as to what I'm able to do." Lou H.

"I golf and do a lot of reading. I joined Chapter Two, a group for widows, where we have once-monthly outings. We'll go to dinner, the opera, a concert series, things like that. I sing in the church choir." Judie N.

"I took up golf. A salesman who came in my store was teaching golf classes. I learned the basics, and it's helped me so many times. I loved singing in the church choir, the concert choir. I loved traveling with my second husband. After he died, I went to Brazil for twelve days to see a dear friend." Marijo Z.

"I enjoy playing pickleball. Before my husband died, I took a watercolor class. After he passed, I wasn't sure if I was going to continue with it, but a year later I'm back in the class." Sandy G.

"I took dance lessons and golfed with my girlfriends in Ohio. I do a great deal of traveling with married girlfriends who take lots of 'girl trips' without their husbands. Taking care of my house by myself takes time. I'd like to join a garden club but don't have the time right now. Get physically fit. If you're out of shape, it compounds how miserable you feel now that you're by yourself. Take a painting class even if you have no talent. It reduces stress, is very relaxing, and the hours fly by. Senior citizen centers often have classes. Every three months you should have a plan for a special event or to travel with a friend. It could even be a nice dinner out. That helps you get through the days when you're alone." Lee M.

"I watch TV, read, clean when the mood hits me. I'll get together with friends. I don't shop as much as I did. I belong to a volunteer group at the local animal shelter." Carole C.

"Volunteer. Learn something new every day. Take a course on something you enjoy, for example, cooking. Take a computer course; it's something you need to do. Keep your mind sharp." Evelyn C.

"I belong to the League of Women Voters, do aerobics, golf, read, walk. I'm a Eucharistic minister at our church." Judie A.

"Do things you like to do but haven't been able to do. I'm thinking of volunteering somewhere. I belong to a Red Hat group. I play cards and take line-dancing lessons at the recreation center. After line dancing, some of us will go out to lunch." Jan B.

"There are not enough hours in the day! The days fly by! There are so many things I want to do and enjoy doing. I play bridge. I used to attend women pilots' meetings. I'm active in my garden club and used to judge club events. When I retired, I joined the DAR, the garden club, and traveled wherever I could." Audrey C.

And a final thought:

"Volunteer. Develop a hobby. If you can, get a job which will take up time. Read. If you haven't tried them, adult and artistic coloring books are soothing. You can go to movie matinees on senior discount days. You can take a regular course or even a non-credit course at a tech college for a reasonable fee. Then you can opt out if it's not for you. You can search out groups through the Internet or on Facebook for those who have lost a loved one." Bobbi V.

Ask yourself—

What are my immediate thoughts after reading the chapter "Filling Your Time"?

_____

_____

_____

_____

_____

Were there suggestions in the chapter that I hadn't thought of, and, if so, what were they?

_____

_____

_____

_____

_____

Some suggestions that I could add with regard to filling someone's time would be:

_____

_____

_____

_____

_____

What do I want to remember from this chapter?

_____

_____

_____

_____

_____

CHAPTER 25
Surprise Packages

(Who Would Have Thought...)

In this new phase of your life, you may find yourself experiencing unexpected "gifts," or as I like to call them, "surprise packages." These may be people who had been in your life before your husband passed, but now you've developed a different relationship with them; your gift might be someone you've met since you lost your husband. Your surprise package could even be a new adventure or an event that has occurred. Be open to acknowledging your special gifts whenever, and however, they enter your life.

In Chapter 6 on Family Dynamics, I talked about the close relationship my twenty-year-old great-niece Kayla and I developed over the summer and fall following Pete's passing. We had so much fun talking, watching TV, having dinner, shopping, and just being together. If she hadn't decided to attend college in Milwaukee, that may not have happened since her home is in Minnesota and mine is in Wisconsin. Having family nearby was supportive for her, and spending time with her was a joy for me. Kayla was certainly an unexpected gift.

Developing a closer relationship with Pete's brother Terry and his wife Marcia was another. We shared the highs and lows of the final months of Pete's illness, which strengthened the bonds we already had as in-laws.

For me, the writing of this book channeled my great loss into helping other widows. That was a huge gift. As so many of the women I interviewed told me, when you help others, you'll find that you're also helping yourself.

The friendships I made with the women interviewed for this book were gifts that keep on giving. During our interviews, these women opened their hearts to me as I did to them. From the beginning, we had the common goal of sharing what we had learned with as many women as possible who were just beginning lives without their husbands. Every time I asked someone if she would agree to be interviewed, she would enthusiastically accept my invitation and, more often than not, give me the name of at least one widowed friend whom she assured me would also love to contribute.

These women who have been widowed have received unexpected gifts and want you to be open to "surprise packages" that may be waiting in your future.

"My special gift was finding my second love. After twenty-eight years of being a widow, I married my second husband. He lived around the corner from me and was the father of one of my daughter's friends. He was a good man who had lovingly cared for his cancer-stricken wife. Again, I was blessed to be with someone who shared my way of dealing with painful times and had a positive attitude, even as he was battling the cancer that eventually took his life. The angels in my life—friends who call to see how I'm doing, who take me shopping, to doctor appointments, to run errands—are one of God's greatest gifts to me. Remember to reach out to your angels as you can help them when they need it just as they help you. Having a friend and being a friend is a priceless, treasured gift for both of you!" Gladi B.

"My surprise package was selling my house and moving to a condo. I would have moved sooner if I had known how much I would like it. Another gift was when my friend Shirley entered my life. I cook with her and talk to her. We talk about the past and what I did with my husband. She is a good listener. She has gotten me through rough times I didn't even know I was in. I'm grateful she is there for me. Another gift is the few close single friends of mine who will drive me places." Mary B.

"I met new people. One is a friend at Curves who is divorced, but divorce is also a kind of death. We both work on our health issues and research ways to fight them. It took us two years to learn what health issues we had. I usually meet women who are single." Lou L.

"My gift was becoming closer to a younger cousin of mine. She came into town, and I invited her to stay with me. We had so much fun! I was able to get to know her as an adult, not just as a younger cousin." Kay P.

"One of my gifts was a new beginning. I wasn't expecting to buy a lot and build a house on it two years after my husband died. My second husband came into my life after his cousins who were friends of mine brought him to a Christmas party at my home. He was definitely an unexpected gift. Other gifts are the different people you meet." Debbi C.

"My second husband was my gift. I was a caregiver for an elderly couple who lived across the street from him. I also took care of their house. He saw me outside doing work and wondered if I was their daughter. He's shy but very strong and precise. We helped each other with yardwork. We were married two and a half years after my husband had passed." Bobbi V.

"One of my gifts was becoming involved with Hillsdale College in Minnesota. They had luncheons and speakers in various areas of the country that I attended. When I went on cruises hosted by a local talk show host, I met nice people and became friends with them. You can mingle on a cruise. I traveled and met so many nice people." Barb B.

"That would probably be the man with whom I had a long-term relationship. This is interesting. One year after my husband died, I went to New York City for a long weekend with a girlfriend. There was a woman reading Tarot cards. I was still wearing my wedding ring, but she said I had lost my husband recently. She said there would be someone in my life after I healed. That was twelve years ago. My significant other, who was a close friend of my husband, and I were together for six years before parting ways." Barb W.

"I met another widow at church, and we just clicked. We became close and cry and laugh together." Beverly K.

"I had community at my former church and was used to the vastness of the Catholic community. I tried a new church but I didn't find that. People who go to church are widows and couples. Some of the women I met at church became my friends." Pearl G.

"For me, that would be The Villages, where I moved in Florida. Ten years ago I would have said, 'Absolutely not!' to living there. Yet, here I am. You don't have to have a partner here. There are many activities like day trips, for example, for you to go on. Everyone is friendly. You have a choice as to what you want to do. No matter where you live, you don't have to stay in the house alone." Angie O.

"I enjoy traveling with my brothers and sister-in-law. I love the bonding time with them. Now that my son is an adult, my husband and I could have done that together." Joanne W.

"I feel the Lord has opened so many doors for me. I'm on the church council and have traveled with my church group. I started a blog. I've become closer to people I had known before." Joyce B.

"Take opportunities that present themselves to do things. Instead of saying you can't do something, ask yourself, *Why not?* I've met lots of new friends. I've had experiences I never dreamed I would have. My boss and his wife took me on a cruise. I went on another fun cruise with other women." Kathy H.

"The joy I found in rejoining the Methodist church was wonderful. A woman there asked if I wanted to join the Women's Circle. I went, she introduced me to other people, and I slowly met more people at church. I even met people there who had known my parents. There was a prayer chain for me when I had my heart operation. These new friends have been such a blessing." Nancy J.

"The other day on my husband's birthday, my nieces texted me to say they were thinking of me. It was so sweet of them." Kay P.

"My puppy Maggie is my unexpected gift. She has brought me so much joy." Judie N.

"My gifts are joining writing groups, singing groups, and golfing." Marijo Z.

"My new friend Nora and I knew the same people, but we hadn't done things together. Then she asked me to go to Albuquerque, New Mexico, to play pickleball with her in the Senior Olympics, and I'm going. We'll play in the seventy-five to seventy-eight-year-old age range. Her friendship came out of the blue." Sandy G.

"On Christmas Eve, my son's closest friend gave me a dozen yellow roses. Yellow roses were the flowers my husband and I loved." Evelyn C.

"I became closer to my girl cousins. We had always celebrated Christmas together, but now they have taken over hosting it. We have fun together, and I started joining them for dinner." Lila S.

"I've become closer to my 'coffee' friends. We go out for breakfast or lunch twice a week." Carole C.

"This was a literal surprise package. My daughter's future daughter-in-law's parents sent me a gift package. It contained different cookies, olives, cheeses, three bottles of wine, crackers, and gourmet popcorn. It was totally unexpected and amazing to receive. On St. Patrick's Day my daughter came over with a bouquet of flowers. It was lovely." Audrey C.

"After the Arlington National Cemetery service when my husband's ashes were interred, my stepson and his wife gave me a lovely throw and a purse. It was so nice of them and so unexpected." Jan B.

And a final thought:

"I had two unexpected surprises. I thought my grandchildren were too busy with their careers to have children. Then my granddaughter had twin girls after my husband (her grandfather) passed and named one of them Poppy, the name she always called her grandfather." Ruby C.

Ask yourself—

What are my immediate thoughts after reading the chapter on "Surprise Packages"?

_____

_____

_____

_____

_____

Have I had any surprise packages that have come into my life since my husband passed, and, if so, what are they?

_____

_____

_____

_____

_____

What advice would I give someone regarding surprise packages?

_____

_____

_____

_____

_____

What do I want to remember from this chapter?

_____

_____

_____

_____

_____

CHAPTER 26
Finding Peace & Joy

Yes, It Really Is Within Your Grasp

If someone asked, "Do you want peace and joy in your life?" what would you answer? It's one thing to say, "Yes, of course, I want that," but it's another to do everything within your power to make it happen. Peace and joy will come to you only if you tell yourself this is what you want. You really do have the power to achieve this.

There are many ways in which I find peace and joy. My Catholic religion and my faith in an afterlife have given me peace and the joyful anticipation that when I pass, I will be reunited with Pete. If I didn't have that promise of seeing him again, I wouldn't be handling his passing as well as I am.

I've mentioned before that I feel love is the connection between Heaven and Earth, and Pete's love fills my heart every day. Your husband's passing isn't the end of the love between you. That love and the memories you have are too strong to die.

I'm open to signs that Pete is still watching over me and am joyful when I see them. My cats Riley and Murphy bring me joy and, yes, peace when I'm petting them and hear their purrs. Letting go of any regrets and concentrating on the good memories will allow peace to enter your heart and soul, as it does mine.

Surround yourself with people who give off positive energy and want the best for you. Those who are negative will be roadblocks to your finding peace and joy in your life.

Asking for advice and help when needed will ease stress. People want to help you; let them know when it's needed. Take into consideration your mental, physical, emotional, and spiritual health. Don't rush making major decisions.

Fill your time with worthwhile activities that take you out of the house. Reach out to those who need comforting. By helping others, you'll be helping yourself. Others have survived losses, and you will, too. You're stronger than you realize, but let that strength come through; don't let your grief create a barrier.

In this book we've given you tips, advice, and stories meant to encourage you and help you make the most of your new life. Always remember that you're not alone. We've been where you are; we've come through the sadness, and it's possible for you to do the same. Remember, you have the power to choose a path of peace and joy.

The women who have been widowed and were interviewed for this book have found peace and joy in their lives and want you to achieve that, as well.

"Think of three happy memories and write them down on a piece of paper. Put the paper inside a cabinet or drawer. When you're having a bad day, take out the paper and read it. Start a journal, and in it write your 'wish list' of things you want to do and your good memories. Page through it to remind yourself of good things." Debbi C.

"This depends on your beliefs and experiences. You may be hurting so much that you can't help others. If you have a religious affiliation, that would help, or you can rely on friends and talk to them about your loss. Remember, there's always someone who has it worse than you. If you realize that you've made a mistake, pick yourself up and move on." Bobbi V.

"Don't isolate yourself. Don't be afraid to do things with friends. Don't hesitate to have friends younger than you. Friends my age are going into assisted living facilities or dying. When you're retired and alone, you need to get out and do things. People may not make calls, so you need to make the calls. Religion has been my salvation." Barb B.

"Remember all the good times, the fun times. Look at photos and remember the fun you had together. Reading uplifting books is beneficial. My faith helps me find peace and joy. Our church has many groups. I went to church camp and had so much fun with the children there." Kay P.

"I'm generally a happy person. Try not to feel guilty because the stress of taking care of someone has been lifted.

"Thinking of the good memories will sustain you and make you smile." Lila S.

"I do my Daily Devotionals. Having a personal relationship with the Lord gives me peace and joy." Beverly K.

"Give yourself permission to acknowledge your pain when something is painful. Get as much wisdom and knowledge as you can online or at the library." Pearl G.

"I say a prayer to God every night that if I'm supposed to find someone, God will send him to me. Having a pet helps you find peace and joy, especially if you're not social. You'll always have someone to touch and talk to. Don't watch a lot of sad movies or TV shows. Develop a new identity. You're a new person, not a couple anymore. For me, that's getting a new place with a garden. Remember, you cannot rely on one person to supply all the needs you have in your life. You have different friends for different needs." Lee M.

"Find your own peace and joy. Don't expect someone else to make you happy; that's not their job. If I'm having an unhappy moment, I'll stay away from people until it passes because I don't want to make others unhappy." Angie O.

"Forget the 'what ifs' and the 'should haves.' Do what makes you feel good about yourself, what makes you happy. Don't look back unless it's to remember the fun times, for example, the hand holding." Joanne W.

"Helping others gives me comfort. For me, it's my faith, drawing closer to God. When you have someone in Heaven,

Heaven becomes closer. This life is not the end; it's a brief moment." Joyce B.

"Always be who you are. Don't change for anyone. Don't let your husband's death define who you are for the rest of your life. You never know when you'll be dealt a bad hand, so try to experience new things." Kathy H.

"I find joy in everything. I love babysitting for my three- and four-year-old great-granddaughters. In my high school yearbook, my teachers called me Smiley. You have to keep a positive outlook even when it's not the easiest thing to do." Shirley W.

"Live each day. We don't know what tomorrow will bring. Get involved with friends. Be happy each day. I'm not calling the kids every day; they'll call me. Be as independent as you can be." Ginny G.

"The whole answer is to get involved. It brings more out of you, and you're not alone anymore, even if you have children. The women I'm meeting have been widowed and are looking for friends. We go to have coffee. If I would get injured, I could depend on them. Helping someone else helps you and makes you feel better. Making a phone call to see how someone else is doing is good for them and for you, too. You forget about your own problems. You're really helping yourself by helping others." Nancy J.

"Get out and do things. If you're feeling down, tell your-self to snap out of it and go to the grocery store. Think of your blessings. Always find something positive. Get together with good friends. The ladies I work out with at Curves are good friends and go for coffee on Mondays and Thursdays, so I always knew I had something to do if I wanted to go out." Kay J.

"You have to get out with old friends, if possible, or meet new people." Jan B.

"Do things with positive people. Get involved with groups. My Wisconsin Red Hat group was a strong support system for me when my husband was sick. You can join a group that knits caps or scarves for those who need them. How you deal with being a widow is more or less how you've always dealt with life. Being in the house too much closes you off from life. You can volunteer to be a 'rocker' for drug-addicted newborns because so many are born to drug-addicted mothers." Carol L.

"You have to look at things differently because you're no longer sharing joy with your husband. Be more open to finding new ways to experience joy. I find that hanging out with other widows is better for me. I giggle more." Lou H.

"Learn to accept what God has given you." Judie N.

"Find someone or something you enjoy. Be glad you're still here. I'm glad that I'm still around to support my daughter, who split with her partner of twelve years." Marijo Z.

"My cats and my dog bring me great peace and joy. Spend more time with others. I'm a former librarian, so book talks or book clubs bring me joy." Carole C.

"You'll never forget him, but now it's your time. I mean that in the sense that now you have to do what makes you happy. Life goes on. You have to move forward. You can't live in the past." Lyn L.

"Look to the future, and enjoy every day. Think of your glass as being half full with all the good things." Joan A.

"Keep laughing. Ask yourself, *What can I do to make myself smile?* Find joy in every day." Ruby C.

"This goes back to my church upbringing. My church is my rock and my salvation in my day-to-day life. You can't give peace and joy to someone who doesn't have it. You have to find it for yourself. Seek some sort of spiritual resource or you can take a yoga class or dance or sing. When you help others, you help yourself. Put yourself out there. Get involved in things you're curious about. Maybe take a class in painting at a senior center. Try doing what you never had a chance to do. Through church, you could take trips, take people to the bank or shopping. Anne Lindbergh said (and I'm paraphrasing here), 'Take risks. If you fail, you will have tried. If you're successful, you will have succeeded.'" Audrey C.

And a final thought:

"The way to finding peace and joy is to accept this is now your life, that these are the cards you've been dealt. The sooner you accept this, the better. The lack of peace in healing comes from you not accepting what has happened.

It's like walking out into a hallway, and the door locks behind you. You keep shaking the doorknob on the door that's locked. What you're doing is missing all the unlocked doors in the hallway. If you don't like what's behind one unlocked door, you can move on. Once you accept this is the life you have, peace comes naturally, and you can move on. There's no timeline. It can happen quickly, or it can take longer for peace and contentment to come back. You're swimming towards shore, and you may tread water at times in between the strokes, but keep heading to that shore." Barb W.

Dear Reader,

If you're feeling the same way that I am as you finish this book, it's as if you're saying goodbye after an emotional, but loving day spent with caring friends who have only one goal in mind, to help you with what they've learned on their journey. This isn't a final goodbye. Anytime you feel the need, all you have to do is open the pages of this book to find all of us waiting for you.

Love,

Bonnie

Ask yourself—

What are my immediate thoughts after reading the chapter "Finding Peace and Joy"?

_____

_____

_____

_____

_____

I intend to find peace and joy in my life by:

_____

_____

_____

_____

_____

My advice to someone seeking peace and joy after her loss would be:

_____

_____

_____

_____

_____

What I want to remember most about this chapter is:

_____

_____

_____

_____

_____

Tips, advice, and stories that I want to carry with me after reading this book are:

_____

_____

_____

_____

_____

_____

_____

_____

_____

_____

Information for the Reader on the Women Quoted

Angie O.—My husband and I were married for forty-nine and a half years when he passed. He died suddenly of a heart attack, although he had heart problems in the past. He was sixty-nine at the time of his death, and I was almost seventy. I've been widowed for ten years and have two sons.

Audrey C.—We were married for sixty-nine years. My husband's death was age-related; he was ninety-two, but his pacemaker had given him extra time. His death was expected, longed for. He was frustrated at not being able to do everything he wanted to do. We were both ready for his passing. I was eighty-eight when he died eight months ago. I have two sons and two daughters.

Barb B.—We were married just short of forty-five years. My husband died of heart failure. He had lung cancer, but it was in remission, which is why his death was unexpected. He was sixty-nine, and I was almost sixty-eight when he passed. I've been widowed for fourteen years. We had no children.

Barb W.—My husband and I were married for thirty-four years. He had been on the heart transplant waiting list for five years and then had another heart attack. His death was sudden. He was fifty-five, and I was fifty-four. I've been wid-owed for sixteen years. We had no children.

Beverly K.—We were married for forty-five years. My husband had been ill with glioblastoma for two and a half years, but he died suddenly of a possible aneurysm while sleeping. He was seventy-three, and I was sixty-eight. I've been widowed for nine years and have two sons.

Bobbi V.—I was married for twenty years. My husband died of idiopathic pulmonary fibrosis (respiratory failure). His death was expected eventually because he had a ter-minal disease, but he died unexpectedly. He passed at fifty-eight, and I was fifty-five. I was widowed eleven years ago. I had two sons and a daughter from my first marriage. One of my sons recently passed. I remarried two and a half years after being widowed.

Carol L.—I was married for almost fifty-one years. My husband's heart just gave out, and his death was expected. He was eighty-five when he passed, and I was seventy-five. I've been widowed for thirteen years and have two sons and one daughter.

Carole C.—I was married for fifty years. My husband died from a stroke after shoveling snow, so his death was sudden. We were both seventy years old when he died. I've been widowed for twelve years and have two sons.

Debbi C.—My husband and I were married for fourteen years. He had non-Hodgkin's lymphoma, and his death was expected. He was fifty-three when he passed, and I was forty-two. I had been widowed for six years when I remarried. I have one stepdaughter and one stepson from my first marriage, and two stepsons from my second.

Evelyn C.—I'd been married for forty-nine and three-quarter years when my husband died of stage four esophageal cancer. It was seventeen months from the time he was diagnosed until he passed. My husband was seventy, and I was sixty-eight. I've been widowed for four years and have one son.

Ginny G.—We were married for eighteen years. My husband died of stage four lung cancer. His death was unexpected, one year after he had been diagnosed. He was sixty-six, and I was fifty-nine. I've been widowed for fifteen years and have one daughter and one son.

Gladi B.—I've been widowed twice. My first husband was my high school sweetheart. We had been married for twenty-two years when he died of a sudden heart attack at forty-four years of age. I was forty-three, and we had four children, two daughters and two sons. I'd been widowed for twenty-eight years when I married my second husband, whose death was expected when he passed away at ninety-two of lung cancer. That was three years ago when I was eighty-six. I also have a stepson and stepdaughter from my second marriage.

Jan B.—I've been widowed twice. My first husband and I had been married for thirty-six years when he died at fifty-six of lung cancer. His death may have been expected, but I was not ready for it. We thought we'd have more time but then learned the cancer was in both lungs. I was fifty-three, and we had three sons. My second husband and I were married two years after I'd been widowed. We were married for thirty years when he died at ninety-three years old. He had heart problems, so his death was expected. I was eighty-five when he passed. I've been widowed now for two years. I have three stepchildren from my second husband.

Joan A.—My husband and I were married for fifty-five years. He died from atrial fibrillation and was in critical condition for the final four weeks. He was eighty-eight years old when he passed and I was seventy-eight. I have three daughters and have been widowed just nine months.

Joanne W.—We were married for almost thirty years. My husband died of a sudden heart attack on the first night of our family's Florida vacation. My husband was sixty, and I was fifty-seven when he passed. I've been widowed for sixteen years and have one son.

Jolene M.—We had been married for thirty-one years when my husband died suddenly of a stroke at sixty-five. I was sixty when he passed, and I've been widowed for four and a half years. We had no children.

Joyce B.—My husband and I were married for twenty-three years. His death was expected from pancreatic cancer. He was seventy, and I was fifty-four when he passed. I've been widowed for two and a half years and have a stepson and stepdaughter.

Judie N.—We were married for forty-seven years. He passed away fairly suddenly due to atrial fibrillation at seventy-five. I was seventy-three. I've been widowed for eleven months and have three daughters—mine, his, and ours.

Karen C.—We were married for fifty-five years when my husband died suddenly of a brain tumor. He was almost seventy-seven, and I was seventy-six. My husband passed away five and a half months ago. I have two daughters.

Kathy H.—My husband and I were married for thirty-five years. He died fourteen months after he was diagnosed with glioblastoma (brain cancer), and his death was expected. He was sixty-three, and I was fifty-five and a half when he passed. I was widowed for thirteen years and met my second husband seven years after being widowed. We were married two years after we met. I have three sons, one stepson, and one stepdaughter. I don't call them stepchildren; I call them "ready-mades."

Kay J.—We were married for sixty-four years. My husband's death was heart-related. We went to bed, and when I woke up, he was gone. His death was very sudden. He was eighty-four, as was I. I've been widowed two and a half years and have two daughters and one son.

Kay P.—We were married for forty-nine years. My husband was diagnosed with stage four melanoma, and he died fourteen months after getting that diagnosis. His death was expected. He was sixty-six, and I was sixty-seven. I've been widowed for thirteen years and have three sons and one daughter.

Lee M.—We were married for twenty years before my husband died from Parkinson's disease. He struggled for four years, so his death was expected. He was eighty-two when he passed, and I was sixty-seven. I've been widowed for eight years. We had no children together, but I do have two stepsons and one stepdaughter.

Lila S.—My husband and I were married for forty-four years. He died of heart disease and complications of diabetes. His death was expected as he had had two open heart surgeries. He was sixty-six, and I was sixty-three when he passed. In three months, I will have been widowed for nine years. I have one son and one daughter.

Lou H.—We were married for thirty-eight years. My husband died of acute myeloid leukemia. His death, four days after he entered hospice, was sudden because we had always hoped for a cure. He was sixty-two, and I was sixty. I've been widowed for nine years and have one daughter.

Lyn L.—We were married for ten years. My husband died of a sudden heart attack and was sixty-two when he passed. I was fifty-nine. I've been widowed for ten years and have one adult daughter. Two years after my husband passed, his doctor, a widower, and I began a relationship that lasted eight years before he died of a stroke.

Marijo Z.—I've been widowed twice. My first husband and I were married for seventeen years. He died of leukemia at thirty-nine, and his death was expected. I was thirty-eight at the time. Four years later, I married my second husband.

We were married for ten months when he died suddenly, at fifty-two, in a car/train crash that also killed my eleven-year-old daughter, my thirty-eight-year-old stepdaughter, and my twelve-year-old stepgranddaughter. I was the only survivor. I was forty-two and have now been widowed for thirty-five years. Two years after my second husband passed, I remarried and am now divorced. I have three living children.

Mary B.—We were married for fifty-six years before my husband died at seventy-six of myelodysplastic syndrome. His death was expected as he had fought the disease for several years. I was seventy-four when he passed. I've been widowed for nine years and have four sons.

Nancy J.—My husband passed away three months before what would have been our fiftieth wedding anniversary. He had had the flu, which turned into pneumonia, and he died suddenly at home. He was seventy-one, and I was seventy. I've been widowed for twelve years and have three sons and one daughter.

Pearl G.—We were married for forty-two years. His death was expected as he was suffering from mesothelioma. He was sixty-five years old, and I was sixty. I've been widowed for eleven years and have two daughters and one son.

Ruby C.—My husband and I were married for sixty-seven years. He had cancer, and his death was expected. He and I were both eighty-seven. I've been widowed for two years and have three daughters.

Sandy G.—We were married for fifty-three years. My husband's death was sudden. He wasn't feeling well, went to the doctor, and was diagnosed with stage four cancer. He was seventy-six, as was I, when he passed. I've been widowed for one and a half years and have one daughter and two sons.

Sherry J.—My husband and I were married for forty-three years. His death was sudden. He died of lung cancer and had been ill for only three weeks and three days. He was sixty-nine when he passed, and I was sixty-six. I've been widowed for thirteen years and have two daughters and one son.

Shirley W.—We were married for forty-two years and had dated for seven. He died of congestive heart failure, and his death was expected. He was eighty-five, and I was seventy-seven. I've been widowed for six and a half years and have one son, one daughter, and one stepson.